CHRYSALIS TAROT

by Toney Brooks and Holly Sierra

U.S. GAMES
SYSTEMS, INC.

U.S. GAMES SYSTEMS, INC. • STAMFORD, CT 06902 USA

U.S. GAMES
SYSTEMS, INC

Published by
U.S. GAMES SYSTEMS, INC.
179 Ludlow Street, Stamford, CT 06902 USA
203-353-8400 • Order Desk 800-544-2637 • FAX 203-353-8431
www.usgamesinc.com

TABLE OF CONTENTS

ABOUT the
COVER ILLUSTRATION

For the cover, Holly designed a cosmic version of our Nine of Spirals, a card that features Aeolus, Master of the Four Winds. Wind itself is a symbol of Cosmic Breath, prana or Spirit, the primary attributes of Vayu, the Indo-Iranian wind god. Wind also symbolizes the power of continuous creation and the forging of harmony between the incompleteness of that which was and the fullness of that which shall be. The Greek god Aeolus is the Great Cosmic Organizer.

One of Chrysalis Tarot's tenets is belief in an emerging Aquarian paradigm characterized by unprecedented change. Aeolus, therefore, represents a perhaps overdue reexamination of your own worldview. He ushers in a new belief system distinguished by cooperation rather than competition, of wholeness rather than separateness, and of cosmic consciousness and a rational spirituality unbounded by stale materialist thinking. He is, in short, the perfect icon for the book you are holding.

FOREWORD

When the Chrysalis Tarot was awarded the Tarosophist Award 2014 for Best New Deck, it received plaudits for its accessibility, vibrancy and novelty, particularly with regard to its alternate naming of the Court Cards and the suits. Others praised its diversity and scope by its incorporation of the widest range of myths, images and pantheons. I fell in love with the brilliance of the deck—both in colour and concept. So I was delighted to be asked to write a foreword for this companion book.

My first experience with the Chrysalis Tarot was remarkable. I often get asked about productivity, and how one can sustain a highly creative life whilst also managing everyday life in the mundane world. I decided to turn to the Chrysalis and pull one card to test its ability to immediately answer a real question. The card I drew from the deck was the Empress.

Whilst I was familiar with its usual interpretations, the image created by Toney Brooks and Holly Sierra provided a rich field of further meaning. In it I saw first that she was drawn as Gaia, and the Little White Booklet (LWB) spoke of the card as representing new ideas and beginnings. However, the depth of the image also provided several creatures; the snail, bringing patience; the mouse, bringing trust; the butterfly, bringing transformation, and also a flower—the Lotus Flower, signifying purity of heart.

These living symbols are found in summary in the simple Robins eggs within a nest cradled by Gaia herself. So I was able to discover that creativity is an entirely natural process when we attune ourselves and trust the world, have patience in it, and co-create our own abundance, as the LWB suggests to us. In this companion book we see how much of the deck teaches the lessons of the Personal Transformation Movement, of alignment, mindfulness and attunement to the vibrations of life itself.

I began to appreciate this gentle wisdom of the deck as I used it for self-discovery and insight into matters both mystical and mundane. I was also able to appreciate how it wove seamlessly the spiritual essentials drawn in other decks, particularly the presence of the *Shekinah*, such an intrinsic yet barely mentioned mystery of the Waite-Smith and Waite-Trinick Tarot images. I am impressed by how such concepts are here raised from religious constraints and placed in a space from which we can all draw, universally and compassionately, through the images of the deck.

Toney and Holly have indeed set out with this deck to transform tarot by opening it out to a wider world and range of interpretation. In this companion book you will learn about the relationship of all things in all symbols; a living universe and rich tapestry that is found in the deck. You will experience with your readings that you are connected to this tapestry in both subtle and direct ways.

Tarot, when most profound, takes us entirely out of time. As the authors say to us; "We are all connected. This means not only everything in the *present* universe is connected, but everything that has *ever existed* in the universe in the *past* is also connected."

In this book, you will also read about Anne Baring's *Dream of the Cosmos* and one particular dream in which she encountered the vision of the net and the spinning wheel. These motifs are to be found throughout the deck in various guises, as they speak of that interconnectivity and timelessness which is at the true heart of all mystical and spiritual experience.

The deck calls us to explore a living universe, not a dead one. As we read, "In a living universe, separateness is an illusion. Everything in a living universe is interconnected, independent and woven into the fabric of a cosmic web of life." I agree here that in a dead universe, tarot would be nothing more than a card game—for tarot to work it must exist in a timeless and connected space, one which is woven invisibly into this world. As we say here at Tarosophy Towers, tarot must be to "engage life, not escape it."

In fact, Toney has written elsewhere on our shared vision to "restore the spiritual dignity of tarot," and it is this vision that you will find deeply written into every card and every line of this book.

The deck is also shamanic, particularly with regard to its healing and holistic intent. The authors see healing as "an incremental aspect of spiritual growth" and much work goes on in the chrysalis, if we are to change and heal. We see this clearly in the Healer card, the Page of Mirrors, a renamed Page of Cups, where we should "collect honey from the many blossoms of your experience and turn it into a mystical balm of healing." I believe too that we all grow "strong in our broken places," to quote the title of the Alice Miller book on the subject of healing childhood trauma.

Whilst the mindfulness of the deck may take us to self-awareness and encourage transformation through recognition of the synchronicity of life, the deck is not without representation of the shadow side of life. The Five of Spirals is here found showing "the repressed feelings of resentment, unhealthy desires and self-centredness or greed." In this book, we discover more about shadow work, incorporating compassion, unconditional love, and personal accountability. Most of all, we come to learn about forgiveness, about letting go by acknowledging and utilising these aspects of our experience.

Profound transformation may unsettle those embarked on such a journey. This deck and book is an effective companion in guiding you through a labyrinth of not only discovery, but towards a destination—a destination which is the centre of your being, the connection between your spirit and matter.

Tarot is above all about story-telling, and this is a story-tellers' deck, a deck aware of tradition and the importance of passing on a tradition with the transformation necessary to reach each generation. These cards are new pictures for ancient stories, and those stories are still those we tell ourselves every day. Our ancestors are written into us and we use our tarot to access their wisdom.

During this hero's journey, the quest for higher consciousness, you will encounter what Toney and Holly have cast as "the Troupe." These are the Chrysalis counterparts to the standard Court Cards in tarot. It appears that these were the most "talkative" of the cards, and they all certainly have a role to play, from the Acrobat (Page of Pentacles) who is our messenger, to the Watcher (Queen of Cups) who speaks of mysticism and contemplation.

I wonder which member of the Troupe will call you to follow them in their journey.

My favourite member of the Troupe—and perhaps this tells you something about me—is the Page of Scrolls, here named the Pilgrim. She shares certain of the shamanic qualities you will discover throughout the deck, and is someone who is able to embark on a journey with a load upon her back. She stands on the doorway between the worlds, having been—or about to be—experienced in both worlds. She is the mendicant, the voyager, the journeyer, and the deck unfolds before her like the wings of a butterfly, promising not only transformation but flight.

Many are the characters we will meet on the way, drawn from Arthurian myth; ancient civilisations; the Celts and Romans, the vast continents of Africa and Australia; but most of all, drawn deeply from our primal selves. This journey is a story of each of us, told on the grand scale but also on a personal stage, in which the spotlight falls upon us.

Tarot tells a story; it is a fable of the soul's only fallacy; that there is something between us and the universe, between our own self and the divine. As we approach that realisation, the cards unfold before us in a constant message; we live a life of service like the Storyteller or Hermit card; we are each Oneida, the *Shamanka*, healing and using tarot to connect us to all stories. Every question, every situation for which we read our cards, is an opportunity for invoking rejuvenation and restoration in our lives and the lives of our querents.

This deck is indeed a story-tellers deck. This book is for learning to read stories in the world through our cards. It marches to a different drum and it is important that we are "aware of the stories that we read and tell," because these stories shape our world. Tarot should be dangerous in that it should change us, challenge us, uplift us and empower us.

I leave you now in the capable hands of the *Chrysalis Tarot*, recalling that "a tarot deck after all is a metaphysical looking-glass, designed to pinch the higher realms of reality."

Tali Goodwin, Tarosophy Towers, April 2015

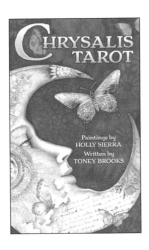

INTRODUCTION

by Toney Brooks

The creation of a tarot deck is a transpersonal process that can take years. Holly Sierra and I spent over 3 1/2 years creating Chrysalis and during those months learned many things. Above all else, we learned that our creative process stood on invisible shoulders.

During the 42 months we spent co-creating Chrysalis, I personally had frequent, imaginary conversations with the characters in our *dramatis personae*. In retrospect, I realize the conversations were not so imaginary after all, at least not entirely. So I embarked on an effort to understand more about what actually went on. This two-part book is not only about Chrysalis Tarot but is also the result of my efforts to uncover hidden realities of the universe that shape our lives and compel us toward destiny.

The most talkative of our characters during the process, and perhaps now as well, were the members of the Troupe. These 16 cards are Chrysalis Tarot's stand-ins for the familiar Court Cards—the kings, queens and so on. Since our Troupe characters were new creations, we expected they might be a wordy lot and have many suggestions to offer. Their suggestions, by the way, were immensely helpful. In effect these characters defined themselves, revealed their personalities and disclosed their functions within Chrysalis. It became readily apparent that the Troupe characters were also archetypes.

Archetypes are pure potential that acquire meaning, definition and resonance through us. Since many Chrysalis archetypes are new to tarot, they learn about themselves just as the universe and everything in it learns about itself: through a feedback, feedforward information (energy) loop. This energy-based network connects everything in our universe, and therefore unifies everything synergistically. The network is holistic and greater than the sum of its parts.

A tarot deck after all is a metaphysical looking-glass designed to pinch the higher realms of reality. In this regard, tarot is a good deal like shamanism. This companion book will acquaint you with the higher realm we call the Otherworld and, hopefully, help you befriend it, learn to communicate with it and listen to it. Hopefully, you will allow the Otherworld to inform you just as you, in turn, inform it. Given the crazed world we live in today, there can be no better time to expand your mind, grow the quality of your consciousness and reexamine your views on the nature of reality.

I personally believe that if something unseen or imagined resonates with consciousness then it is real. Any author who creates a character that subsequently becomes an archetype, such as George Lucas' Darth Vader, will tell you the character is indeed very real. As you write, characters say and do things that surprise the writer. Our mythologies are filled with living characters that resonated in the past and now, as archetypes, transport treasured truths into future ages from one to the next.

Today, perhaps more so than ever before, we humans inhabit a compacted reality in a wounded world. Every time we think we have it completely figured out, we realize that we only found another piece of the puzzle. Today's cobbled together puzzle is defined by the primacy of matter, separation, and duality, which is a polarity of opposites in pairs such as masculine vs. feminine, good vs. evil, light vs. darkness and separate vs. unified. Unreconciled opposites and the fallacy of separation are egocentric illusions that beget war, pestilence and senseless destruction of planet Earth.

Fortunately, reality isn't set in stone; we changed our perception of it before and we can change it again. Our human nature intuits when profound change is blowing in the wind and readies us to make sense of it. Today, the world around us is experiencing birth pangs that herald a new reality and worldview. What possibly could be more exciting than to experience the birth of a global awakening?

Our unique deck of 78 tarot cards was crafted to help midwife this new existential reality, a reality we describe at times as *holistic consciousness* and at other times as *cosmic consciousness*. They imply the same thing. We symbolize this new consciousness throughout Chrysalis Tarot with beautiful butterflies and striking symbols of personal transformation. Chrysalis marches to a different drum. It seeks to help you forge a pathway to destiny and cosmic consciousness. The pathway is the ageless Hero's Journey, the monomythic quest for unity.

Holistic consciousness, a dimension of higher consciousness, resonates at the highest possible frequency because it is characterized by pure, unconditional love—immaculate love for self, neighbor, the Earth and the Cosmos. The new reality awaiting the conclusion of the Hero's Journey is an experience of spirit *and* matter; unity *and* separateness, divine Self *and* divine other. The philosophy of the new age prefers the term *both/and* rather than *either/or*.

Profound change is unsettling and frustrating, especially to those ill prepared for it. We designed Chrysalis Tarot to help mitigate the stressful tremors of troubled times. When we evolve our understanding of reality and learn to abide by it, we are able to lower the inevitable stress brought about by change.

So what exactly is going on in this world of ours? That's a question we put to Chrysalis cards. We asked, "Who shall represent these winds of change?" The Nine of Spirals responded. This card depicts the ancient wind god Aeolus who symbolizes cosmic organization. Wind itself symbolizes the invisible spiritual energy that forges new paradigms. Humanity has been on the cusp of this new paradigm, or new age, since the Enlightenment of the 17th century.

Aeolus is pictured on the Nine of Spirals with an astrolabe, a device used at sea for navigation. An astrolabe measures not the speed or direction of the wind, but rather the position of heavenly bodies such as the moon and stars. On the Nine of Spirals, the astrolabe foresees the gentle breeze of the Age of Aquarius entwined with the last snarling gusts of the Age of Pisces. The ramifications of such a shift are stupendous!

Our universe is made of vibrating energy. All that exists in the universe is "energy, frequency and vibration," according to the renowned physicist Nicholas Tesla. All matter is vibrating energy. This book, for example, vibrates at a specific frequency. The furniture around you vibrates at a specific frequency. And your personal energy vibration or *energy signature*, which is affected by your mood and state of mind, broadcasts a specific frequency. Personal energy signatures *resonate* when they come into contact with complementary frequencies, such as other like-minded individuals.

To visualize resonance, imagine a tuning fork. When you tap it, it produces sound at a specific frequency. Say you have two identical tuning forks and you tap one of them, the other fork vibrates at the same frequency and you can hear it.

A radio also comes in handy when visualizing resonance. We know radio stations broadcast on assigned frequencies. When a radio set is tuned to a particular station, the station's frequency resonates with the radio, which then produces sound you hear through the speakers. If you change frequencies by pushing a button, the sound from a different station begins to resonate.

This companion book to Chrysalis Tarot details a mental and spiritual journey of resonating frequencies. Tarot refers to this journey as *The Hero's Journey,* a catchall that has been a feature of humanity's stories and mythologies since the time of Gilgamesh nearly 5,000 years ago. In our own time, the whole of humanity is embarking on an epic journey of self-discovery and a collective re-examination of values and priorities. Once accomplished, this paradigm shift will redefine humanity's role in a living universe.

This book divides this epic journey into two parts. Part One examines Chrysalis Tarot and other forms of magic, which are the manipulation of subtle energy, and the role they play in the epic. We will examine new ways of thinking. By opening minds, we will learn how the universe really works. Much of what we were taught in school is incorrect. In just the last several decades, new ways of thinking opened the frontier for a New Physics and New Science that present a much clearer and more elegant view of the way the world works.

Part Two of this book provides an in-depth interpretation for each of the 78 Chrysalis cards. The interpretations also include anecdotes written by Holly that include her inspiration for each card's art with images of her original black and white sketches.

In Chapter 1, titled *Elpi's Cosmic Insights*, we'll review, in layman's terms, the New Physics and various scientific discoveries that turned our worldview upside down and inside out.

We'll examine two different views of the universe. The present view is of a cold, mysterious, foreboding place created out of nothing some 14 billion years ago. The greater universe, aside from our own solar system, doesn't appear to serve much purpose or to have much direct bearing on everyday life on Earth in this worldview. We've been taught that it's mostly dead, empty space.

The alternative, and I believe correct view of the universe, differs considerably. While it may indeed appear cold and foreboding, it most certainly is not dead, empty space.

In Chapter 2, *Papa Legba's Unseen Travels* expands upon what we at Chrysalis call the Otherworld, or Collective Unconscious. Chrysalis archetypes depicted on the first 22 cards in the deck are said to exist in this Otherworld, a realm of non-ordinary reality. As we mentioned, the 16 Troupe characters also inhabit this Otherworld.

When a particular Otherworld archetype resonates with your unconscious mind, your imagination and intuition are inspired. You know new things inexplicably. The tarot reading becomes something like a radio that's happened upon an unfamiliar but entertaining station chocked full of information.

Chapter 3, *Merlin's Great Matter,* addresses resonance and the transformation to higher consciousness, the ultimate goal of the Hero's Journey. The word *chrysalis* itself implies either biological metamorphosis or spiritual transformation.

When you read Chrysalis Tarot, you invite the Otherworld into your daily decision-making and discernment to help you make better informed choices. You also become happier, less stressed, more confident, better balanced and, as the frequency of your energy signature rises, so too does consciousness awareness.

We devote Chapter 4, titled *Storyteller's Vision Quest,* to healing. Diseases may be *cured*, psychological disorders may be *treated*, but when subtle energy vibrations become disordered they must be *healed*. Various names for what is called *subtle energy* include *chi* (also spelled qi) and *prana*, the Sanskrit word meaning "life force." This energy is subtle only because we lack the technology to measure it.

We'll also discuss the etiology of subtle energy disorder, the telltale symptoms of illness one might encounter and the many effective healing modalities available, which includes Chrysalis readings. We also touch upon chakra work and other forms of subtle energy healing.

Chapter 5 is titled *Morgan's Cauldron of Rebirth*. Morgan le Fay is Chrysalis' sorceress. It's about the magic that happens when you activate your Third Eye, also known as your sixth chakra.

An activated Third Eye stabilizes your frequency so it may resonate *at will* with the unseen world of archetypes and discarnate beings, such as spirits, angels and the ancestors. Fairies, unicorns and fantastical creatures from mythology also populate this imaginal Third Eye theater.

Perhaps of utmost importance, when consciousness is tuned to this stabilized frequency you will also resonate on many levels with fellow human beings committed to evolving beyond the dead-universe materialist paradigm.

Part Two of the book expands on interpretations of Chrysalis cards detailed in the small booklet (Little White Booklet) that comes with each deck. In addition to the card interpretations, Holly's inspirations for her Chrysalis art are included along with her original black and white sketches for all 78 cards.

The card descriptions in Part Two refer to the finished cards—the beautifully colored images of Chrysalis Tarot. In several instances, the black and white sketches do not include all the features and symbolism found on the finished product. Examples include Elpi's scarf (you can't quite make it out), the tree on the Four of Stones (it isn't there), and the animal familiar on the Dreamer (which was changed). We apologize if this is confusing. The idea behind including Holly's original sketches was to show how the artistic process evolved inside the chrysalis.

PART ONE

CHAPTER 1

ELPI'S COSMIC INSIGHTS

If you want to find the secrets of the universe, think in terms of energy, frequency and vibration. ~ Nikola Tesla

If you haven't already met Elpi, she's the archetype pictured on our version of tarot's traditional Star card. Elpi herself is a minor deity from Greek mythology. As the personification of hope, Elpi remained behind when Pandora opened the jar known to us as Pandora's Box. Pandora's curiosity allowed good and evil to escape into the world. Aesop tells us, "Elpi is still found among the people promising she will one day bestow upon them all the good things that got away."

Each evening, and true to that promise, Elpi keeps hope alive by flying into the heavens to coax the stars from their daytime hiding spots and set them ablaze with her Golden Censor. Nightly treks across the Milky Way have taught Elpi a great deal about the true nature of the Cosmos. That's valuable information that will help us understand how tarot works. It also provides a cosmological framework for the new living universe paradigm.

Elpi's job was rather simple back in the days of Aristotle, when the universe was thought to be a finite sphere. Stars adorned the ceiling— the sphere's outermost boundary. After the Copernican Revolution an astrologer named Giordano Bruno, who was also a monk, put forward the radical notion that the universe knew no boundaries. It was infinite. The stars were other suns, perhaps even orbited by planets similar to planet Earth.

At the beginning of the 20th century, the existing worldview was overthrown once more, this time by Relativity and Quantum Mechanics. For the first time in human history no comprehensive mythology or scientific worldview could neatly explain everything. But Elpi assures us there is hope.

ELPI'S ENERGY SIGNATURE

Contrary to popular belief, the universe is not empty space. It's true that the observable matter in the universe accounts for only about 4% of the stuff in outer space, but the remaining 96% is not empty. It's filled with small packets of energy called quanta. This energy can be imagined as tiny vibrating bubbles.

"Empty space," incredibly, contains more energy than everything else in the observable universe combined. Considering there are 100 billion galaxies in our universe each with over 100 billion stars, that tallies up to a massive amount of "empty space" energy.

It's important for us to learn about this vibrating energy because it accounts for how tarot, the interconnectivity of everything in the universe, and perhaps even consciousness itself, actually work.

This energy is called zero point energy, *prana*, *chi* or *aether*, among other terms. It occupies not just all the empty space in the known universe, but also all the empty space inside every atom—and that's a lot of empty space too. Atoms themselves are 99% empty space; therefore you, me and all matter are comprised of 99% empty space. But we're also vital links in a dynamical system that connects everything in the universe to everything else.

Elpi's energy signature vibrates at a specific frequency. If emotions are hopeful, positive and optimistic, energy signatures vibrate at a high frequency. If Chrysalis archetypes like Elpi evoke positive vibrations, they are said to *resonate* with us. But let's say we're having a slightly off day and aren't feeling very hopeful. Our energy then vibrates at a significantly lower frequency. Love has the highest vibration frequency. Fear, on the other hand, vibrates at a very low frequency in the same range as anger and hate.

With the twinkle of a distant star that's Elpi's energy signature. The more you believe Chrysalis Tarot cards are a lot more than beautiful pieces of cardboard, and the more you energize them with your own positive thoughts, the greater the effect will be on a card's resonance, and hence its ability to lift your spirits and heal your psyche.

THE DEAD UNIVERSE WORLDVIEW

Perhaps the greatest obstacle to viewing the universe holistically is the physics of the existing dead universe worldview that divides the universe into two broad groupings: the large objects we can see like planets, stars and galaxies; and the small objects that account for everything else, such as atoms and protons that we can't see.

Classical physics explains the big things; quantum physics explains the small things. Since there is no widely accepted "theory of everything" combining a rational spirituality with science, we naturally view the universe as a dead universe having little relevance to everyday life on Earth.

The dead universe worldview is responsible for many of the problems we face today on planet Earth. Here's today's conventional wisdom that goes to the heart of the matter: Inanimate matter is considered to be dead. The visible universe is made of matter that has no purpose. Matter has no consciousness. In a nutshell, this perspective describes the material worldview, the worldview of a dead, meaningless, fragmented universe. Put another way, the universe is a machine.

In a dead universe, tarot can be nothing more than a card game. Meditation and yoga are self-indulgent "Eastern" folderals. Everything in a dead universe is matter made of particles that obey mechanical and physical laws. Everything that is real can either be seen or measured. In a dead universe, there is no room for metaphysics, tarot or other anomalistic phenomena such as extrasensory perception, near death experiences or energy healing. In a dead universe, such notions as these are considered insubstantial and ephemeral.

Today's dead universe worldview legitimizes wholesale exploitation of the planet, wars for control of Earth's natural resources, plus a lack of sincere compassion for other humans. Worst of all, separation and contrived political and religious boundaries bolster the notion of a dead universe, separating us from nature and from each other.

THE LIVING UNIVERSE WORLDVIEW

When Elpi streaks through the heavens each evening she sails on a veritable sea of fluctuating subatomic energy. We can't see this energy, but then neither can a fish in the ocean grasp the vastness of the water it swims in. As we noted, one cubic centimeter of space contains more total energy than all matter in the known universe combined, according to physicist Nassim Haramein. The energy from one cubic centimeter of space could power everything on Earth for years!

In a living universe, separateness is an illusion. Everything in a living universe is interconnected, interdependent and woven into the fabric of a cosmic web of life. We no longer regard the world as a place of objects but as a place of relationships. We view Earth through the holistic lens of deep ecology where the whole is greater than the sum of its parts and each part has the responsibility to preserve the vitality of the whole. In a living universe, we evolve from a model of competition to one of cooperation. In a living universe, everyone matters.

These notions are incremental to understanding not only reality but understanding tarot and other forms of anomalistic phenomena. We'll further examine this subject in Chapter 5, *Morgan's Cauldron of Rebirth*.

THE COSMIC WOMAN

We conclude Elpi's chapter on the cosmos with the story of a life-changing dream that author Anne Baring recounts in her magnum opus, *The Dream of the Cosmos*. Baring dreamt she fell into a deep valley and landed in a vast net somewhat like a spider's web. When she raised her eyes she beheld a beautiful "Cosmic Woman" who seemed to fill the entire cosmos. The woman had an immense, revolving wheel in her abdomen that reminded Baring of the famous labyrinth at Chartres Cathedral.

Of course, the wheel is a universal symbol for the spinning cycles of birth, death and rebirth as well as a symbol of the Mother Goddess. The wheel's cosmic energy permeates all planes of existence. It also symbolizes the body's seven chakra centers of consciousness, which are discussed in the following chapter.

When Baring glanced down at her own body, she discovered she too had a revolving wheel, except hers was slightly askew to the left. The Cosmic Woman indicated to her that her wheel should also be centered, although she didn't indicate how to go about doing it.

Centering the wheel, Baring later realized, meant becoming fully conscious and aligning her own human consciousness with the woman's superior cosmic consciousness, who she now recognized as a personification of the Divine Feminine. Baring also recognized the net in her dream as Indra's Net, a sutra from Hindu mythology and prominent symbol of the interconnectedness of creation.

Stephen Mitchell further explains Indra's Net in his book *The Enlightened Mind:* "The Net of Indra is a profound and subtle metaphor for the structure of reality. Imagine a vast net; at each crossing point there is a jewel; each jewel is perfectly clear and reflects all the other jewels in the net, the way two mirrors placed opposite each other will reflect an image ad infinitum. The jewel in this metaphor stands for an individual being, or an individual consciousness, or a cell or an atom. Every jewel is intimately connected with all other jewels in the universe, and a change in one jewel means a change, however slight, in every other jewel."

CHAPTER 2

PAPA LEGBA'S UNSEEN TRAVELS

One cannot help but be in awe when one contemplates the mysteries of eternity, of life, of the marvelous structure of reality. It is enough if one tries to comprehend only a little of this mystery every day.
~ Albert Einstein

Papa Legba is the Grand Shaman of Chrysalis Tarot. He can frequently be found in liminal space—the betwixt-and-between of the crossroads that separate the visible realities of the world from the invisible realities of the universe. Liminal space is the threshold between what we experience through our five senses and what we experience though intuition, dreams and active or creative imagination.

Other shamanic spirit guides in Papa's entourage include Storyteller, Celtic Owl, Ariadne, the Watcher and the Visionary, however many other cards also have shamanic attributes, such as the Nine of Stones, Eight of Mirrors and the Pilgrim. Additionally, threads of shamanism are woven throughout the Chrysalis fabric by our weavers, the Seven of Mirrors and the Weaver. When any shamanic styled cards appear in a reading, it confirms resonance and a strong connectivity with the Collective Unconscious, which we call the Otherworld. We could say that Chrysalis was heavily influenced by shamanism.

THE COLLECTIVE UNCONSCIOUS

In order to comprehend the vastness and meaningfulness of the Collective Unconscious, it is first necessary to grasp the full implication of the living universe axiom: "We are all connected." It means that not only everything in the *present* universe is connected, but that everything that ever existed in the universe is also connected. The Collective Unconscious is a living system of connectivity and a dynamic memory bank.

The Collective Unconscious is also a dynamic energy field whose organizing principles are universal archetypes such as those pictured on tarot's 22 Major Arcana cards. In the case of Chrysalis Tarot, we consider the 16 members of the Troupe also to be archetypes.

The Collective Unconscious is often referred to by other names such as the Akashic Record, Cosmic Mind or Universal Mind. However conceptualized, the Collective Unconscious can be summed up as the confluence of world mythology and spiritual tradition. Chrysalis honors all these traditions with a rich holistic cultural diversity.

In the alchemy of Chrysalis Tarot, a reading represents spiritual resonance with the Collective Unconscious that takes the form of intuitive dialog. The specific purpose of such dialog is to increase your knowledge of Self.

A COSMIC TOUR WITH PAPA LEGBA

In the previous chapter we discussed empty space, which quantum theory proves is not empty at all but filled with energy. This energy was called *aether* until the early 20th century. Space indeed is filled with a super-dense, superfluid energy awash with an infinite number of fields of information. One of these fields is the Collective Unconscious.

Renowned scientist Sir Arthur Eddington wrote, "To put the conclusion crudely, the stuff of the world is mind-stuff." There are several promising theories that propose space is not only full of energy but is also full of consciousness. A cornerstone of the living universe theory is that consciousness is nonlocal. In other words, consciousness does not arise from matter (the brain), but is pervasive throughout the universe. Consciousness can be called the Ground of All Being.

Philosopher Ervin László reported that in altered states of consciousness (ASC), "Many people experience a kind of consciousness that appears to be that of the universe itself." Such altered, non-ordinary states of consciousness could also explain near-death experiences, out-of-body experiences and, of particular relevance to us, how tarot readers *connect* with the Collective Unconscious and evolve to the state of *cosmic consciousness*.

A giant step in the evolution of consciousness is anticipated by the Aquarian paradigm.

GAIA

Another dynamic energy field in space particularly relevant to users of Chrysalis Tarot is the Gaia Theory of Mother Earth. James Lovelock developed his revolutionary Gaia Hypothesis in the 1960s. It asserts that the Earth is a living, self-regulating organism that maintains optimal conditions to support life in our biosphere, one of Earth's four geologic subsystems. Lovelock's hypothesis has become a scientific theory named Gaia Theory.

Gaia's energy field also sheds some light on the extensive array of ley lines (earth energy meridians) and sacred monuments that dot the landscape in many areas of the globe. Indeed, our Ace of Stones depicts a menhir or megalithic standing stone. Even today many consider sacred megaliths (large stones) to be unimportant curiosities constructed by "primitive" ancient civilizations. Like religion, archaeology is blindly dogmatic about these matters.

Morphic resonance is a hypothesis conceived by biologist Rupert Sheldrake in the late 1960s. It theorizes that memory is not stored in the brain but is inherent in nature and all natural systems. Future generations depend not so much on inherited traits as on the collective memory from previous generations—an information system similar to the Collective Unconscious. Morphic resonance benefits all species of life.

Morphic resonance is relevant to Chrysalis because it accounts for the strong influence our ancestors have in tarot readings and day-to-day life. Indeed, there are specific cards in Chrysalis designed to represent and call upon ancestral energies. These include the Four and Eight of Spirals.

COSMIC CONSCIOUSNESS AND WHY IT'S VITAL

Rumi wrote, "In form you are the microcosm; in reality you are the macrocosm." Is that endearing platitude or scientific fact? Well, it's both. As human beings, we can be described as a microcosm; the living parts of a greater whole. But in reality, we are not only connected to all other living parts but to the totality of the whole, which exists in the center of our being. When the Great Cosmic Woman appeared to Anne Baring that was the essence of her message: by centering ourselves and tuning our consciousness we become one with all the information contained in the cosmos. We are both microcosm and macrocosm, as Rumi wrote.

When designing Chrysalis Tarot, Holly and I agreed on several objectives. We wanted a deck that promoted *mindfulness* because mindfulness increases synchronicity in our lives as well as self-awareness. We wanted a *healing* deck because healing is an incremental aspect of spiritual growth; one must become whole to grow spiritually. The healing efficacy of Chrysalis Tarot resides in its shamanic qualities and energy. But most of all we wanted a deck that would evolve consciousness and be *transformative*.

We wanted Chrysalis to be aligned with the Personal Transformation Movement. This movement includes yoga, meditation and other centering and grounding methods, along with an acute environmental awareness. The Personal Transformation Movement seeks to end *competitive* "us vs. them" thinking in favor of a *collaborative* model that is holistic and interdependent.

If there's a stumbling block to cosmic consciousness, it is the fact we have never had an accurate model of how the universe actually works. A person's worldview, which must include cosmology, up to now has been a mixture of mythology, metaphor and science. This mixture has been stultified by dogma, both religious and scientific. It's little wonder we see ourselves as separate from the universe and from one another; there are too many fragments and divisions, the antithesis of holism and Oneness.

Cosmic consciousness anticipates replacing belief-based dogmatic versions of reality and science-based dogmatic versions of reality with a foundational vision that transcends both. Moreover, to heal divisions and end the illusion of separation with a paradigm that explains how things really are.

EXPERIENTIAL SPIRITUALITY

One great advantage tarot holds as a tool for personal transformation is that it does not depend on memorizing correct beliefs, rather it relies on empowering personal experience. When traveling through the unseen world with Papa Legba, we experience a sense of the numinous, which is far more rewarding and instructive than reading someone else's account of their experience. Their experience is their truth, not yours. Chrysalis Tarot actively seeks to create such an experience of the numinous (Collective Unconscious) for our readers to help them discover their own personal truths.

Spiritual alchemy is defined as a conversation with the numinous. It is the hallmark of every Chrysalis reading, meditative exercise, chakra clearing and transpersonal ritual. As you progress in spiritual awareness and learn to journey deeper and deeper into the center of your being, you will hear echoes from great sages; you will transcend boundaries of ordinary physical reality and discover the holy grail of true happiness and compassionate well-being.

– CHAPTER 3 –

MERLIN'S GREAT MATTER

According to this mythology there is no fixed law, no established knowledge of god, set up by prophets or priests that can stand against the revelation of a life lived with integrity in the spirit of its own brave truth.
~ Joseph Campbell

In the quote above, Campbell, the world's best-known mythologist, references the Quest for the Holy Grail, which he termed "the founding myth of Western Civilization." Grail mythology lies at the heart of the Hero's Journey, the journey of self-discovery that leads to spiritual transformation—the journey that is the essence of tarot.

In Chrysalis Tarot, our journey begins with Merlin who, in his stand-in role as the archetype of Self, accompanies and guides you on your own personal Hero's Journey through the cards. Merlin, the mystic and legendary guardian of the Holy Grail, is the world's best-known spiritual alchemist. The Quest for the Holy Grail as told by Chrysalis is Merlin's Great Matter and your *summum bonum* or highest good. The Grail legends are about growth, which is the reason we are here.

Merlin plays the role of your alter ego or best friend forever in Chrysalis. In every reading, Merlin the Mystic stands at your side to coach, comfort and nudge you forward. He speaks through your inner voice, your robust imagination and inspired intuition. The two most important qualities on the Hero's Journey are active imagination and mindful attentiveness. This way, you can't possibly miss a thing.

THE HOLY GRAIL

Grail legends trace their roots to the 5th century, a tumultuous period in British and Celtic history. No longer able to "defend the limes," Rome's auspicious legions were yanked out of Britain. Within only a few years the Saxons, Angles and other tribes invaded from across the channel. This sent many native Britons reeling and fleeing to safety in the Celtic countries of Ireland, Wales, Cornwall, Scotland and Brittany. What history calls the Dark Ages began when Rome abandoned British soil.

The Dark Ages were dark because the history of the period was not recorded in written form; the northern peoples were storytellers and kept oral histories. Stories were told and proud legends embellished about a young king named Arthur and his mentor, Merlin. They halted the Anglo-Saxon advance in Wessex at the Battle of Badon Hill and thereby ushered in a long period of peace called the Golden Age of Camelot. Our humble Chrysalis Merlin was cut from the same cloth as his famous namesake—he desires only what is best for you and always eschews personal glory.

By the High Middle Ages writers such as Geoffrey of Monmouth, Chrétien de Troyes, (1100s), Wolfram von Eschenbach (1300s) and Thomas Malory (1400s) had turned the Grail and Arthurian stories into the legends we know and revere today. More than anything else, the lesson of Camelot is one of peace not war, collaboration not conflict and equality not domination. King Arthur's Camelot was characterized by brave knights, chivalry and courtly romance.

Joseph Campbell wrote in *The Power of Myth* that the foundational substance of myth is message, not fact. The timeless message of Arthurian and Grail legend is clear: the overarching quest for over a thousand years before Camelot and for over a thousand years since has been the quest to achieve yin/yang balance on a global scale; the quest to return and re-enshrine the Divine Feminine, the virgin essence of the Holy Grail that was woefully exiled from our own souls.

Author and mystic Anne Baring equates spiritual pathology in the modern era to the exile of the Divine Feminine and the corresponding loss of soul individually and collectively. She writes, "The masculine principle becomes pathologically exaggerated [and] inflated...the symptoms are rigidity, dogmatic inflexibility, omnipotence, and an obsession with or addiction to power and control."

The feminine principal on the other hand does not exaggerate in the opposite direction. The feminine principal is one of yin/yang balance.

THE CELTIC CAULDRON OF REBIRTH

The Grail first appeared in the written literature of medieval France, although the source of Grail stories is much older. The word itself was first written as *gral* and referred to a serving dish. In her book *Grail Alchemy*, Mara Freeman noted the Grail "belongs to a family of symbols—bowl, cauldron, vat, well, cup, or crucible—that are all images of the Divine Feminine … as far back as the Neolithic era [stone age]."

In Chrysalis Tarot, the Troupe—our Court Card replacements—symbolize the faint echoes of a distant past. In the 12th century, a troubadour would carry news and gossip from village to village in what is now the pastoral French countryside but was then Celtic Brittany. It's the troubadours we can thank for planting the seeds that flowered into the Arthurian Grail legends cherished today. The compendium of this bountiful bouquet of courtly legend became known in literary circles as the *Matter of Britain*.

Above all else, Grail legends provide compelling metaphors for human development and spiritual growth. The Quest for the Holy Grail can be thought of as a quest involving soul recovery—aspects of the psyche or soul, individually and collectively, that went missing when the Divine Feminine was exiled. As Mara Freeman phrased it, "The Grail stories arose when Western religion had been dominated by male god-forms for over a thousand years."

The Quest is thought of as the hero's triumph of Authentic Self over unauthentic ego. The Quest for the Holy Grail becomes not only a personal quest for self-discovery but also a quest to reintegrate the Divine Feminine into the Western psyche individually and collectively.

The inseparable spiritual objectives of soul recovery and reintegration exist in today's world. They are the alchemical reagents of the magical crackling and bubbling we see in Morgan le Fay's Cauldron of Rebirth. The magic of Morgan's sorcery is soul recovery, which can only be accomplished fully with the rebirth of the Divine Feminine in our time. In Chrysalis Tarot these inseparable individual and collective quests are known as Merlin's Great Matter.

RETURN OF THE SHEKINAH

The word *Shekinah* means indwelling or resting place. In kabbalah mysticism the Shekinah represents the feminine aspect of the divine, which has lived in sorrowful exile for over 2,500 years. All mythological pantheons in one form or another include a personified reflection of the Shekinah. She has been called Sophia, Durga, Quan Yin, Danu, Isis, Nokomis, Hecate, and many other names.

In Chrysalis Tarot, the principle of the divine feminine has little or nothing to do with religious worship or correct beliefs; we regard religious dogma as the entropy of genuine spirituality. The Shekinah is symbolized in Chrysalis as the Great Mother and Moon archetype, which exemplifies her unassuming, maternal qualities and profound connection with the Collective Unconscious, which often is symbolized by a churning sea.

The Shekinah is directly implied by three cards that comprise Chrysalis' Triple Goddess archetype: Ariadne (maiden), Gaia (mother) and Storyteller (crone). The Divine Feminine may be inferred by several other cards including Ma'at, the Muse and the Weaver.

The exile of the Shekinah finds its cultural analog in the separation of the cosmic soul (Psyche) from human conscious awareness (ego). This is a predictable consequence of a materialist worldview that insists upon the primacy of matter and pigeonholes consciousness as a mere function of matter—specifically, a function of the gray matter inside the human skull.

In contrast, Chrysalis regards consciousness as a nonlocal phenomenon that is both fundamental and omnipresent throughout the cosmos. Consciousness in our schema is defined as the "Ground of All Being," a concept articulated by Dr. Amit Goswami, a theoretical quantum physicist. Goswami exclaimed this realization was "the most exalted experience in thought I ever had."

Chrysalis regards the human brain as a dynamic processor in a system that forms a universal feedback-feedforward loop of ever increasing complexity. As Hamlet said, "There are more *things*, Horatio, in heaven and earth than are dreamt of in your philosophy." As we transition from the Piscean to the Aquarian Age, these "things," the incomprehensible mysteries Shakespeare wrote about, are being explained by quantum physics.

The cybernetic (how systems communicate) feedback-feedforward loop, in which the human brain and consciousness play such vital roles, is the process that permits the universe to increase in complexity and consciousness; to learn about itself and evolve. The system permits life on Earth to contribute to the evolution of life throughout the cosmos, an awesome responsibility.

Tarot, meditation, yoga and others consciousness raising endeavors also contribute significantly. The bridge linking the personal unconscious to the Collective Unconscious is also a cybernetic feedback-feedforward loop; we learn from the archetypes and evolve our spiritual awareness; the archetypes in turn learn from us and similarly evolve. This feedback-feedforward process is presented visually on the Two of Spirals card.

Merlin's Great Matter foretells the global-scale reintegration of the Divine Feminine in the human psyche, an event that presages an unprecedented quantum leap in human consciousness. As your friend and guide during your Hero's Journey through Chrysalis, Merlin and his cohort of benevolent archetypes will assist in tuning your conscious awareness to the future resonance of the Aquarian Age.

Because we expect this punctuated increase to happen soon, we chose the first three cards of Chrysalis Tarot very carefully. The triad of Merlin, the Ravens and the Sorceress Morgan le Fay assures the proper mixture of bold magic and plucky mischief to accompany you on your quest to locate the Celtic Cauldron of Rebirth and your personal destiny.

CHAPTER 4

STORYTELLER'S VISION QUEST

Beware of the stories you read or tell; subtly, at night, beneath the
waters of consciousness, they are altering your world.
~ Ben Okri, Nigerian poet and author

Our Storyteller is an Oneida shamanka, a female shaman schooled in the ways of the holistic Wise Women. As a traditional healer, she radiates and manipulates the Earth-centered energy symbolized by many Chrysalis Tarot cards. Tarot, to a certain extent, is similar to meditation, yoga, and reiki—all set as their goals spiritual growth and healing. As a healing modality, tarot emphasizes the sacred ideals of self-knowledge and self-acceptance. As a whole, Chrysalis cards encourage shadow work, forgiveness, compassion, unconditional love, personal accountability, mindfulness, unity and the sanctity of life.

These vibration-raising ideals are essential to the health of body, mind and spirit. The most powerful healing the human body experiences is the remarkable internal energy of its own rejuvenation and restoration. Whenever she is prayerfully invoked or appears in a reading, Storyteller breathes her healing balm. Like all shamans, she lives the quiet life of compassionate service to others.

In addition to psychological and emotional healing, Chrysalis promotes energy attunements that are fundamental to the fields of complementary and alternative medicine. Storyteller and her people call this subtle healing energy *Orinda*, an Iroquois word she learned on her grandmother's lap as a small, frail child. The Anishinabes call it *Manitou*, but we're likely more familiar with terms like prana, chi or qi. They all refer to the same thing—a vast web of vibrating energy that pervades the Cosmos and connects everything in it.

Storyteller's grandmother also taught her that Orinda connects us to our ancestors through an energy field the First Nation anthropomorphized as "The Grandfathers." Chrysalis refers to this field as the Collective Unconscious or Otherworld. It is home to not only Storyteller's Oneida ancestors, but also to the universal archetypes that are part of everyone.

Storyteller's ancestors learned about frequency, vibration and resonance, although the terminology differed during the trying times and tribulations of the Fifth Fire, a time when the worlds of the Iroquois and Anishinabe changed forever. After the prophecy of the Fifth Fire had been fulfilled, the stories were passed down through generations forever stained by the blood and tears of those terrible times when the ancestors abandoned the old ways. But the ways of the shaman never changed. These were the stories told by Storyteller's grandmother. They were healing stories that never change.

Many times Storyteller was told about Polly Cooper and her Oneida compatriots who bravely carried food to George Washington's starving soldiers at Valley Forge in the bitter cold winter of 1777. As a little girl, she traveled from Wisconsin to New York with her grandmother on a pilgrimage to venerate the famous shawl Martha Washington gave to Polly. That proud account became a healing story Storyteller herself told often. As a sickly child, Storyteller learned to overcome adversity that made her strong and who she is today. She often remarks, "Pain and adversity produce growth."

Now grown old and well into the eventide of her memories, Storyteller recalls the Oneida legends that came to define her life. They are legends of courage, ingenuity and perseverance. A thousand words are nestled comfortably in her mind like gemstones mined from sacred verse and hewn from sacred time. When later recalled, her memories enrich her life in ways even she finds hardly imaginable.

The word Oneida means "people of the standing stone." Standing stones are monuments that mark the permanent sacredness of Earth's energy meridians. Chrysalis features standing stones and other megaliths on many cards that tap symbolically into rivers and streams of Earth's healing energy.

SHAMANISM

The shaman is an adept manipulator of subtle energy, as are all practitioners who work with what we call *resonance*. We define resonance as the ability to tune into ethereal (delicate) frequencies associated with subtle energy. You perceive these frequencies each time a tarot card resonates with you.

These extra-sensory abilities are present in everyone, but may be better developed and attuned by some individuals. It takes practice. Shamans, for example, spend years developing and honing their unique calling and skill set. The shaman's path can be likened to the Hero's Journey, which is an inward journey into one's own center. In humans, this center is the heart chakra. The new Storyteller sketch at the beginning of this chapter depicts Storyteller's healing orb as her heart chakra.

In western mysticism, three states of spiritual growth are generally recognized. They are the initiate, the illuminate and the adept. Teresa of Avila, a famous mystic, drew an analogy between watering a garden and these three spiritual states or phases.

She explained that an initiate draws water from the well and carries the buckets into the garden. An illuminate digs a network of trenches to irrigate the garden. The adept simply walks into the garden and it begins to rain.

Chrysalis Tarot was designed to encourage you to plant a garden and, for starters, grab a bucket or two. Merlin, as your constant guide and trusted confidant, is also a consummate rainmaker. He guides tarot initiates through the Chrysalis process of transformation. Chrysalis adepts are called Psyche or butterflies. The words have the same meaning in Greek.

We'll leave the analogy there, but it's important to note that chi or prana describe an infinite field of frequencies and resonances. Other energy fields include Gaia, the biospheric feedback feedforward loop that maintains optimal conditions for sustaining life on Earth, as well as more familiar energy fields such as Earth's electromagnetic field and Earth's magnetosphere that protects us from solar radiation.

The auric energy meridians in the body known as chakras are yet another field. The field we tune into the most in tarot is the Collective Unconscious, the equivalent of a timeless human memory bank. Like other fields, the Collective Unconscious contains an infinite number of frequencies.

As human beings we resonate with frequencies borne by pranic energy, the field of information and consciousness that flows through each of us. It connects us to the sea of information that is our universe.

ENERGY AND THE ARCHETYPES

We run across the word *archetype* frequently in tarot circles. Without archetypal energy tarot would be little more than a card game. The overarching concept of archetypes was developed by C.G. Jung. He defined an archetype as an organizing principle in the Collective Unconscious that influences the architecture of human consciousness.

At Chrysalis, we consider, as did Jung, archetypes to be organizing principles, each with its own unique energy signature that can resonate with the human psyche. While an archetype, by definition, is a symbol without form, we individually ascribe coherence to them simply through mutual interaction. In that regard, communication with archetypes becomes a new language—a new form of communication. The more we communicate with archetypes using this language of active imagination and intuition, the more fluent we become in it. Indeed, we even acquire the ability to think in this language, which is a characteristic of synchronicity.

With Chrysalis Tarot this new language includes all 78 cards, not just the archetypes of the Major Arcana. All Chrysalis cards connect with the Otherworld. The Troupe characters (spirit guides) are also archetypes, as are the four Aces plus a significant number of Minor Arcana cards. These include, among others, the Four of Spirals (ancestral hearth), the Seven of Scrolls (counterintuitive reasoning) and the Seven of Mirrors (reclaiming empowerment).

Adding to the excitement of this universal language is a consort of spirit animals that appear throughout the deck. Totemic spirit animals, like archetypes, are important to the healing ministry of shamans and to Storyteller's healing ministry in Chrysalis.

MAGIC IS REAL

While some may scoff at notions of psychic ability, life after death, remote viewing, shared death experiences, precognition and tarot, the fact remains that science, particularly quantum physics, has begun to provide architectural framework to facilitate examination and explanation of these anomalous phenomena.

If Storyteller manipulates pranic energy in order to heal, Morgan le Fay makes magic with it in her cauldron, as we shall discover in the following chapter.

CHAPTER 5

MORGAN'S CAULDRON
OF REBIRTH

*The universe is full of magical things, patiently waiting for
our wits to grow sharper.* ~ Eden Phillpotts

Holly's sketch of the Pythia (shown at right) presents a perfect example of rebirth, recurrent themes and the boundless nature of archetypes without regard for cultural distinctions. An archetype knows no borders; he or she is truly a child of the universe. The Pythia, Morgan le Fay's equally famous Grecian counterpart, is better known as the Oracle at Delphi. The same vapor that wafted through a crack in the rock floor of the Delphian Temple of Apollo is depicted wafting up from Morgan's magical Cauldron of Rebirth on the Chrysalis Major Arcana card titled "Sorceress."

The ancient Greeks called this vapor *pneuma*—the word for breath or spirit, and appended magical qualities to it. Scholars continue to debate whether the vapor was a type of gas that made the Oracle utter gibberish that required an interpretation by priests. That's a dubious claim at best; no one aside from the Pythia seems ever to have been affected by the vapor. Furthermore, the Oracle reportedly spoke clearly and intelligibly according to the late Joseph Fontenrose, a classical scholar and author of the seminal treatise on the Delphi Oracle.

Holly's new Chrysalis sketch of the Pythia is richly symbolic. In her left hand, she holds a laurel sprig from Apollo's sacred tree. In her right hand, she holds a bowl of water dipped from the Castalian spring that flows near the oracle. The water, it's said, contained gases like methane and ethylene, and that the Pythia drank from the bowl. That may account for the poor health of those who served

as the Pythia, but the bowl of water likely was a scrying bowl, the cousin of a crystal ball.

The common thread that ties Pythia and Morgan le Fay together is, of course, the practice of shamanism, which even today is considered by some as a form of magic or supernaturalism. Today, however, we accept *pneuma* as an archaic word for pranic energy.

Today the artful manipulation of pranic energy, a carrier of information, whether effected by healing shamans, prescient clairvoyants or wise oracles, still wafts vapors of magic and the occult. In truth, it's all a matter of skillfully finetuning frequencies that resonate to some degree with everyone, and then simultaneously filtering out other frequencies and the pernicious chatter of the mind.

On Morgan's tarot card we included the Ravens, as Holly did on the new sketch. There's a good reason for that; ravens are tricksters, the essential go-betweens found in all magical traditions. Tricksters prance lively upon the liminal curtain separating the seen and unseen worlds. They are commonly misunderstood and undervalued characters on the world stage. Tricksters play an essential starring role in life.

Tricksters do magic at thresholds and boundaries for which they hold little, if any, regard. They dart across boundaries, disrupt boundaries and sometimes create new boundaries all in order to make the world, shall we say, a more interesting and less predictable place. When the world needs to change, the world turns to tricksters. We could no more excise tricksters from magic than trees from forests or stars from heaven. Tricksters haul away the metaphorical dross from staid cultures and drench moribund energy with pneuma so cultures can regenerate and learn to adapt, thrive and evolve. Tricksters perform the heavy lifting of needed change. They could be called the "hand of the gods."

TAROT AND MAGIC

We can term the art of reading tarot *an experience in magic,* but not in the occult sense of the word. As we noted, there was a time when magic took on weighty occult connotations, but the sun is rapidly setting on those days. Today, magic connotes action, activity and essence that science, for its own reasons, hasn't gathered the wits to explain.

In Chrysalis, the word *magic* means synchronicity—the meaningful coincidences in life that cannot be explained. Since Chrysalis was first published, we discovered it engenders a great deal of synchronicity. One possible explanation is that synchronicity is an echo of the feed-back, feed-forward energy loop we described in the previous chapter. It isn't bound by the customary constraints of time.

Magic seems to happen most often when there's an elevated sense of the present moment, an acute awareness psychologists call *mindfulness*. We can't explain the feeling, but we recognize it when it happens. It's also described as being *in the flow* or having an experience of the numinous. These are exhilarating experiences. Things just seem to come together and fall into place with little or no effort on our part. That's the magic of synchronicity!

SYNCHRONICITY

Synchronicity, the meaningful coincidence of unrelated external and internal events, is spiritual energy that taps you on the shoulder for a particular purpose. That purpose is to inspire you to stay on destiny's path. Synchronous energy can serve to confirm recently made decisions, or decisions being contemplated. Synchronous moments are always meaningful. They let you know you don't walk alone.

Interpreting the meaning of a synchronous message or series of messages with precision is a daunting task requiring objective discernment. Sometimes the meaning is immediate and obvious, whereas on other occasions it doesn't become clear until much later. Meanwhile, just patiently walk with the mystery.

Morgan's cauldron is a melting pot of synchronicity. In Chrysalis, synchronicity is connected mostly with the Major Arcana and the Troupe. But Morgan also mixes up the vibrations of other magical energy in her cauldron. Most prominent among these is fairy energy;

Morgan le Fay is Queen of the Faeries. She also stirs up ancestral energy. The ancestors help us grow in many ways and always look out for us.

GOING WITH THE FLOW

Around 15 years ago, I wrote a book about King Arthur that included Ariadne as a character. She appears in the Celtic pantheon as the Goddess of the Gates of Time and in the Greek pantheon as a daughter of King Minos of Crete. After I finished the book, I decided to travel to Crete to do some firsthand research on the Minoan civilization and Ariadne, who had captured my imagination. At the time, I lived in Cornwall, England and planned to fly to Crete.

As I was booking the flight to Crete, the travel agent's computer froze solid. She exclaimed, "I'm so sorry. This has never happened before!" Being on the lookout for the synchronicity of odd happenstance, I asked, "May I please see your screen?" She swung it around and I immediately noticed a flashing number in the upper right corner—the number 222, which holds a special meaning to me. I asked, "So where is that flight going?" She answered, "To Cyprus." I didn't hesitate: "Please book me a return (roundtrip) to Cyprus." This illustrates an instance of synchronicity seizing and freezing the present moment so we can closely examine it.

The following week when the plane landed in Larnaca, I began the usual exasperating search for a rabbit trail. The trail I eventually found took me down the coast to Limassol and eventually to an archaeological museum there. I admired a number of interesting artifacts in the museum recovered from a dig at Amathus, a short, scenic six-mile bus ride.

Amathus was a beautiful ancient port city but there's hardly anything left of it now save the outlines of the harbor, city walls and the ruins of its marketplace (*agora*). It was one big archaeological excavation site that included its acropolis, which was sacred space to several civilizations during the city's lifespan. Amathus thrived under Phoenician rule some 3,000 years ago. In fact, I learned that Ariadne's name and mythological lineage are likely of Phoenician origin.

I had a high degree of anticipation as I began the bus trip from Limassol to Amathus. I felt synchronicity sent me to Amathus for a reason, but had no idea what it might be. I held no expectations of finding Ariadne there. Her mythology belonged to Crete. I carried a canteen and a guidebook purchased from the museum. It made sense to start at the acropolis and work my way down to the agora.

On the acropolis, the remains of several churches built on top of one another over the years were apparent and provided visual evidence of what takes place when the old gods replace the new. Appropriation of sacred space, and even of saintly individuals, is quite common when religious beliefs change. When Christian missionaries, for example, experienced difficulty abolishing the cult of a pagan deity, they simply stoked the machinery of sainthood. The Celtic Pagan goddess Brigid is known to Christians as St. Brigid, however the cult of the goddess Brigid survives and thrives.

As I wandered around trying to get my bearings, my heart stopped as I spotted this passage in my guidebook: "We should look for a moment at a puzzling feature, a tomb cut in the rock…and almost certainly the earliest thing attributable to human activity in the city. A small flight of steps, oriented exactly north-south, leads down to a narrow corridor and to a roughly circular funeral chamber…The tomb had been remodeled and partly filled in at the beginning of the Archaic Period (800 B.C.E.)," the guidebook matter-of-factly concluded.

It added, "This tomb was known as the Tomb of Ariadne." I was awestruck and became very excited. What was this if not magic? I had no idea I would find Ariadne on Cyprus.

On Crete Ariadne was a princess; on Cyprus she was a goddess. And her cult of worship was actually centered in Amathus! I'm reluctant to admit it, but when I booked the flight to Cyprus, I wasn't exactly sure where in the Mediterranean Cyprus was located.

In retrospect, the Ravens were likely behind the trickster energy that accosted the poor travel agent's computer. Their inspiration likely came from Ariadne herself under her mantle as the Celtic Guardian of the Gates of Time, a title that still resonates strongly with me. I'll always believe she guided me to Cyprus and to that very spot, to her tomb at Amathus.

The magic was quite unmistakably the work of Morgan le Fay. She has redrawn the map of my life on several occasions over the years. She and Ariadne were also responsible for bringing Holly Sierra and I together to create Chrysalis Tarot.

In this way, the Otherworld is always nudging us forward in the direction of destiny, if we allow it. We designed Chrysalis to assist in learning how to let go and allow Otherworldly magic to influence our actions and decisions. I included this story with hope that the magic of Ariadne, Morgan le Fay and Chrysalis Tarot will seize and freeze the present moment often on your own Hero's Journey. *Namaste.*

PART TWO

In Part Two of the Chrysalis Tarot companion book, we take a closer look at the card meanings and the symbolism in the artwork. For each card in the deck, Holly presents her original black and white Chrysalis sketches and offers a glimpse of what inspired the art, shown on the left-hand page. She shares her personal stories of how she chose the characters, figures and settings for the cards. Or how sometimes they chose her!

On the right-hand page are Toney's expanded interpretations of the card meanings. We also explore how each Chrysalis card, with its unique mythos and particular healing energy, helps guide you through the transformational journey toward higher consciousness.

MAJOR ARCANA CARDS

The first 22 cards in a tarot deck are known as the Major Arcana. In Chrysalis we number these cards from 0 to 21. The images on the Major Arcana, called "Majors," represent archetypes from the Collective Unconscious, such as the Hero, the Sun and the Moon. The majors also symbolize masculine and feminine principles, gods and goddesses of different mythologies and their attributes, animals and spiritual concepts that link us to worlds beyond the limitations imposed by our intellect, ego and emotions.

As we explained in Part One, archetypes are coherent patterns of energy-filled images. They communicate with us in two ways. First, they resonate with the unconscious mind and, since energy is dynamic, they do so using an information-sharing feedback-feedforward process. In other words, archetypes engage in conversation with active imagination. This process is known as *spiritual alchemy*—a resonating conversation with the *numinous*. The numinous is the unseen Otherworld.

Conversations with the numinous serve a great purpose. The resonance elevates the unconscious mind into conscious awareness. Alchemical resonance brings about transformation, higher consciousness and a renewed awareness and sense of the wonders of life. Conversations with the numinous assist in discerning important choices that keep us on destiny's path. They improve intuitive skills and help us imagine revolutionary new possibilities.

Exciting additions to the Chrysalis companion book are anecdotes written by Holly about each card. Holly shares with us her artistic inspirations and details her experiences while co-creating Chrysalis.

REVERSALS

Some experienced tarot readers read cards in reversed positions (drawn upside down). This is a divination technique dating to tarot's 18th century beginnings, an era that predates Jungian archetypes and quantum physics.

We don't recommend this method with Chrysalis. While Chrysalis is quite effective when used for divination, it does so without using reversals, which can be confusing to beginners. Chrysalis was primarily designed as a tool to assist with spiritual growth, self-awareness and personal transformation. For a system to be truly spiritual and truly effective, it should be easily accessible to all.

We believe the answers to life's important questions can be found inside us, in our minds and the hearts, and are never encrypted. Holistic (mind, body and spirit) resonance using Chrysalis helps taroists access the answers they need by utilizing their intuition and imagination informed by inspiration from the Otherworld. In Part One of this book we discussed the engine under Chrysalis' hood. In Part Two we put you behind the wheel.

O – MERLIN

When we decided upon Merlin as our hero, the decision immediately brought to mind my explorations at Tintagel on the romantic Cornish coast. Especially memorable, was my trek to Merlin's Cave. It was very atmospheric and one could easily envision Merlin approaching, his cloak glimmering with staff held high to light the darkness of the cave. I wanted our Merlin to appear as the wizards of my childhood did— approachable, loyal, dependable, somewhat wizened but ready for adventure and the task at hand. As I had encountered so many wonderful cats on my adventures in England, I decided a feline made the perfect companion for our sage friend. After Chrysalis' publication, I moved across country to Sedona, Arizona, where I encountered a lovely statue of Merlin in the center of the village. For me this depiction of Chrysalis' Hero encouraged me to begin my new life with renewed faith and high hopes!

Merlin portrays the archetype of the wise old man. Hopefully, he brings new life and high hopes to your readings as you embark upon your own Hero's Journey. Merlin represents your alter ego—a friend, spirit guide and mentor who remains by your side as your interpret Chrysalis cards, whether he should appear in a particular reading or not.

The Hero's Journey is known as a monomyth, a term coined by James Joyce and popularized by Joseph Campbell in his book, *The Hero with a Thousand Faces*. Campbell noted the Hero's myth was found in cultures all over the world. Western Civilization's principal analogue is, of course, *The Odyssey* by Homer.

But unlike Odysseus, who encountered bewitching sirens and two-headed monsters blocking narrow straits, the journey through Chrysalis Tarot encounters a far friendlier Otherworld. There, you'll meet archetypes and universally recognized symbols that successfully see you through life's narrow straits.

When you meet Merlin in a reading, take note of his cat and the snake on his staff. The snake pays tribute to the Egyptian snake goddess Wadjet. She's there to invoke Divine Feminine protection on your journey. One of Wadjet's earliest symbols from 5,000 years ago depicted a cobra coiled around a papyrus stalk, the inspiration for Merlin's healing staff. That motif morphed into the rod of Asclepius, a recognizable symbol used in healthcare today.

But Wadjet isn't the only Egyptian goddess Merlin invokes. His cat is named after the Egyptian cat goddess Bastet. Both Bastet and Wadjet symbolize the Eye of Horus—your all-seeing Third Eye that's associated with your sixth chakra. Ancient Egyptian cats were often adorned with jewels and pampered as household pets.

The Hero's Journey is a struggle for dominance between the irrepressible Ego Self and the Authentic Self. Like the snake goddess Wadjet, those who take the Chrysalis journey shed their old skin to reveal a newly transformed and transfigured Higher Self.

1 – THE RAVENS

*A*h, *the Ravens, or as they've made themselves known to me, the Tricksters. I first saw Huginn and Muninn in an old illustrated manuscript, where they were depicted sitting on Odin's shoulders, bringing him 'pearls' of wisdom and regaling him with tales of their explorations. I loved the aged quality this old depiction held. I decided to have our ravens perched in the Yggdrasil whose branches are filled with designs inspired by my love of fractals. The Ravens 'act up' whenever they get the chance (or so we've found), so when it came to working with their images I naturally encountered many mix-ups, glitches and delays. They are indeed mischievous characters, but I learned that their meddling frequently resulted in my exploring new paths that ended with magical synchronicity!*

We quite naturally associate Merlin with magic. It's implied by his popular moniker, Merlin the Magician. But in truth, Merlin is an alchemist who helped young King Arthur discover his destiny. Spiritual alchemy entails blossoming into full selfhood. And that requires a little magic along the way.

In Chrysalis, the Ravens provide the magic that maneuvers you toward truth and destiny. That's why tricksters were absolutely essential at the beginning of the Chrysalis journey. Tricksters are the "straws that stir the drink."

A trickster is an enigmatic and often misunderstood archetype full of purposeful deception that borders on exasperating disruption. Yet tricksters teach us that by unmasking deception we discover truth. Well-known mythological tricksters include Kokopelli, Loki, Hermes, Coyote and even Shakespeare's Puck. Ravens are the consummate tricksters in mythology.

Our Ravens perch in the high branches of the Yggdrasil—the Norse Tree of Life. The upper branches symbolize a tree's spiritual realm, the Ravens' natural haunt. Trickster magic unfolds as synchronicity. Important signposts often appear magically in life at the proper time and place without requiring a great deal of contorted effort from us.

Like hidden tripwires in the middle of a well-worn path, trickster magic produces bumps in life when you're not being mindful or paying attention. Bumps remind us that we often make things far more difficult than they need to be. Tricksters regard a bump as an opportunity for growth.

The trunk, roots and branches of a tree correlate to body, mind and spirit. The Raven's Third Eye peers out from the heartwood of the tree—the pillar of a tree's experience of life. A tree renews itself from the inside out, from heartwood center to roots and weathered branches. This holds metaphorical meaning. The Ravens teach us that if spiritual renewal proceeds from the heartwood of Higher Self, it produces a positive effect on our physical and emotional well-being.

2 - THE SORCERESS

I *felt very strongly about my depiction of Morgan le Fay as she is
such an evocative, mysterious character. One immediately thinks
of the misty Isle of Avalon and an enchantress with impressive transformative powers. Around the time I began sketches for Morgan, I
made an online friendship with a Croatian girl named Ivana. The
photos she posted of herself put me in mind of how I wanted our
sorceress to appear, so I asked her permission to use one in particular.
And she became our Morgan! I have found it's a powerful way to
proceed because finding the right model makes the end result all the
more realistic and tangible. Lastly, when it came to the background,
rather than go with a more traditional, star-filled sky approach, I felt
the Aurora Borealis might best indicate Morgan's amazing powers.*

Where Morgan is concerned, "amazing powers" is almost an understatement. When you lift the Chrysalis hood, you'll find Morgan's Cauldron of Rebirth. She cooks magic in a crackling eight-cylinder cauldron. Chrysalis, you could say, is "powered by Morgan's magic." Rebirth is an appropriate mantra for this card because rebirth alludes to the butterflies that weave their own threads of magic all through Chrysalis cards.

Morgan le Fay is the Queen of the Faeries and one of the world's best-known sorceresses. Her unique brand of magic is fairy magic, the magic that combines synchronicity and healing. We imagine that also under the Chrysalis hood there are fairies everywhere.

The essence of tarot, as well as for other tools for transformation, is the same—they are the Great Work of alchemy. Spiritual alchemy is defined as a conversation with the numinous. The First Matter, the *prima materia* in alchemy, is the celestial fire of primordial Oneness. Prima materia has been symbolized by many different things over the years. Among them are the Philosopher's Stone, the Serpent, the Dragon, and even the fiery burning water found in magical cauldrons.

A modern interpretation of "fiery burning water" is consciousness evolving into Higher Self coaxed onward by the ravens. Morgan's tableau is dynamic. The scene comes to life with crackling flames beneath the cauldron and dancing colors of an aurora borealis, the electric ballet of the northern skies. In southern skies, this cosmic dance is known as the aurora australis.

Since Chrysalis was published, we have noticed a strong presence of fairy energy in the cards. So much so that we designed a special Fairy Ring Spread that can be found on page 212. The spread is intended to invite fairy energy into our lives and to convey specific intentions to the fairy realm through Morgan le Fay.

If Morgan turns up as your Card of the Day, or if she appears frequently in readings, consider asking the gentle folk to enlighten your life with their wisdom and guidance using the Fairy Ring Spread.

3 – GAIA

*O**ur Gaia is dressed in the garb of summer. Her spirit is intended to make you feel like you've just crossed a hedgerow and entered a sunlit meadow covered in golden grass and ripening seeds. The musical accompaniment is a whisper of soft summer breezes, birdsong and the buzz of honeybees. All about you the heady scent of wildflowers waft in the breeze. Although the Earth's energy is powerful, varied and immense, I chose to portray Gaia as a warm, youthful and welcoming maternal spirit. I painted her during my days of work at the Stowe Art Gallery in Vermont. At one point I discovered that a little mouse was living in the gallery. He was running back and forth in the main salon, so I decided it was a sign that he wanted to be featured in Gaia's world!*

Holly's story ties in wonderfully to Spirit Animal energy, a feature of Chrysalis Tarot and the mystical world of shamanism. Chrysalis cards frequently help you identify your own spirit animal, if you haven't met yours.

A mouse is the perfect spirit animal for Gaia. He's adaptable and pays great attention to detail, like an artist. And like Gaia. She's not only the Greek goddess popularly known as Mother Nature, she's a scientific theory known as Gaia Theory.

With artistic attention to detail and mouse-like adaptability, Gaia insures that optimal conditions to sustain life on planet Earth are always present. Gaia is a dynamic, living system known rather dryly in Earth System science as a cybernetic feedback loop. Gaia's *feedback loops* connect animate and inanimate living systems so that they can share information and co-evolve. Our magnificent planet was sculpted by the nurturing forces of Earth, Fire, Wind and Water, all woven into an interconnected web of activity more exquisite than anyone could possibly imagine.

Gaia is a body that maintains homeostasis. For example, golden dust storms in the Sahara Desert that contain ancient bits of iron and phosphorus are lifted high into the sky by winds. They contain plankton, a micronutrient essential to life. This dust is then propelled by wind across the Atlantic to fertilize the Amazon rainforest, where a fifth of Earth's oxygen is produced.

That is Gaia artfully performing her magic. As stealth as a mouse in an art gallery, she keeps our planet alive so that it and we might thrive. We humans, a fairly recent addition to Earth's fauna and flora, could and should be doing a great deal more to assist her.

In readings, Gaia reminds us to respect the remarkable beauty, glowing abundance and magical artistry that animates and safeguards planet Earth. By doing so, we create an abundance of joy and well-being in our own lives.

4 – GREEN MAN

This card was one of the first paintings I created for Chrysalis, and I must confess he's one of my favorite subjects. I wear a Green Man pendant around my neck at all time that was given to me by my daughter. There are so many representations of our foliate-headed friend that I strived to create a unique rendering for our readers. One day while visiting a friend's garden I was impressed by their ivy groundcover, and it inspired me to think anew. I decided it might be visually interesting to depict our Green Man's features as if they were made from vines as opposed to leaves. His wren companion stands for sharing activity and efficiency, the nest for rebirth and the butterfly for your inner voice.

If Gaia is the artist who paints the natural world, Green Man provides the canvas. He symbolizes the heart and soul of nature. In Celtic legend, Green Man is a vegetation deity, as Holly portrays him. For six months of the calendar year, Green Man is the Oak King, master of the waxing year. For the other six months he's the Holly King directing the final acts of nature's annual birth, death and rebirth performance.

We paid tribute to a little mouse in our remarks about Gaia, so let's pay tribute here to a little wren, Green Man's spirit animal. To the Celtic Druids, the wren was a sacred bird given to singing all day long. Druid priests would pay close attention to the wren's birdsong and interpret it—sacred birds like the wren know many secrets.

Wren is also known as Bran's Sparrow. His namesake is Bran the Blessed, a character from Arthurian legend. Bran's sparrow tells us that wrens are go-to birds because they are bold, resourceful and efficient. In a reading, Green Man himself may be informing you that wren is your spirit animal.

In his fatherly role in Chrysalis, Green Man signifies the unrealized potential and resourcefulness of the human spirit. In readings, he reminds you to live mindfully in the present moment and give thanks daily for nature's cornucopia of abundance.

But above all, Green Man personifies nature's voice, which always speaks to you. His inspirations appear in dreams, memories and our intuition. Green man confirms his role in your life via meaningful coincidences of synchronicity—a gentle puff of wind at an auspicious moment, a birdsong or crow caw or a wispy image in a drifting cloud—these are musical notes in Green Man's loquacious symphony.

Green Man reminds us of a line from William Wordsworth, *"Come forth into the light of things; let nature be your teacher."*

5 – DIVINE CHILD

When Toney first shared his thoughts about the Divine Child I thought it a wonderful exchange for tarot's traditional Hierophant. Having raised my own two 'divine children' I saw how valuable it was for adults to witness children as they begin to grow and embrace the world: Self-acceptance comes naturally and self-discovery follows. We made our Divine Child androgynous; the butterflies symbolize his/her transformation. I had recently visited a 'Butterfly Pavilion' where the beautiful insects were all around and I found it very inspiring visually. It's worth noting too that during my Chrysalis painting days in Vermont many frogs and toads came to our doors and windows. In fact, at one point I had a regular nightly visitor. He seemed inquisitive. I thought he'd make the perfect companion for our Divine Child!

Divine Child's parents are pictured on the next card, the Lovers, at their Sacred Wedding. Divine Child enters the world with Original Grace and nothing separates him or her from the rest of creation; not creed, race, nationality, nor dogmatic religion. Divine Child is a free thinker with unlimited spiritual potential, as represented by the palette. Its brilliant colors symbolize spiritual truth and represent treasures to be experienced. Divine Child would rather find treasures than just read about them.

Divine Child does not enter the world as a *tabula rasa* (blank slate). Far from it! He or she enters bearing a palette of unrealized self-potential and a paint brush for the process C.G. Jung termed *individuation*. A fully individuated human being is one who has recovered destiny—the soul's ultimate purpose and destination.

One of the most difficult challenges we face in life is to embrace and accept our own divinity and unique worthiness. Divine Child embodies the essence of shamanism and the principle of private revelation. She is fully empowered and requires no intermediaries between the guiding spirit of the universe and herself.

As your inner voice, Divine Child frequently whispers reminders that you must paint your own canvas; that you are personally responsible for attaining your own destiny. On your Canvas of Destiny appears a soul sketch drawn by the Collective Unconscious. It is pure and unstained; there is no blemish of any kind.

A soul sketch has a unique property Jung called "the fire within." It's the intuitive force that nudges and guides destiny's brush strokes. What sparks the fire within? The answer: fairytales, mythos and active imagination—the same creative influences that animate Chrysalis Tarot.

In readings, the Divine Child asks you to become a full-time seeker of truth and light your fire within; to blaze your own spiritual trail and reject disempowering delusion by questioning everything with an open mind.

6 – LOVERS

The tree of life reigns supreme here as a symbol of eternal life, connections, love and attraction. Our connections, however short-lived, often remain with us for an eternity. At the time I painted this card I had just purchased a book called Remarkable Trees *(which I highly recommend). In any case, I was put in mind of some of these marvelous old trees when I was sketching Brigid and Arthur. I decided this tree would serve as a sort of crown chakra over our lovers' heads—a Cosmic Consciousness Center to aid in one's 'leap forward' with Merlin's assistance. I included all the animals of the woods, too, because our deck celebrates wildlife. Chrysalis reminds us they are an integral part of our existence and well-being. It's only fitting they would attend the Lovers wedding!*

Our two lovers are none other than King Arthur and Brigid, the Celtic Goddess of Hearth and Home and the Keeper of the Sacred Flame. But this celebration is far more than an ordinary wedding in the woods. It represents the archetype of the Sacred Wedding also known as the *hieros gamos*, an alchemical "union of opposites" not well appreciated today.

In the sacred wedding of Arthur and Brigid, sun and moon are symbolically joined together, opposites are reconciled and made whole (male and female, anima and animus); the two become as one and confer divine grace upon one another. The sacred marriage of Osiris and Isis is another example of the unifying mythology of *hieros gamos*.

Wedding announcements went out to all the creatures of the forest. It was an invitation to a "New Golden Age," symbolized by King Arthur and Brigid's marriage. Both Arthur and Brigid, an epiphany of the Divine Feminine, were exiled thousands of years ago. There was the brief mythological Golden Age of Camelot, but it will not compare with the Golden Age being celebrated here. The last Golden Age of this magnitude occurred in Ancient Egypt around 2500 BCE.

Golden Ages follow paradigm shifts, as we discussed in Part One. In readings, the Lovers extend an invitation to bite the forbidden apple and forsake the cherished worldview of a disconnected, dead universe of nothing but matter. The Golden Age of Aquarius heralds a connected, living universe of consciousness and matter.

The Lovers card in a reading might also symbolize previously shattered aspects of psyche that are now being healed, united and made whole in a celebration of soul recovery. Weddings are joyous occasions, as are Golden Ages. The two greatest healing emotions are love and joy, the emotions conveyed to your reading by the Lovers.

7 – HERNE THE HUNTER

Many nights I sat bundled up outside staring into the cool, crisp darkness of the Vermont sky, marveling at the constellation of Orion. Very prominent above Earth on those midwinter nights, it's one of the brightest and most beautiful of all the constellations. Toney and I had decided to feature the three stars of Orion's Belt in our depiction of Herne. I became very intrigued by Herne and the literary references I'd found describing him. He seemed a terribly romantic but at the same time a formidable figure. In the end, my depiction even scared me a bit. One literary source calls Herne "a spirit and keeper of the forest." *And sometimes through whirling shrouds of mists one spies Herne atop his black steed with hounds and an owl in pursuit. I thought his power must be great!*

Herne the Hunter is an energetic fellow. His energy is the same raw Earth energy we find represented on the Ace of Stones. As this energy resonates through the seven chakras, the body's energy meridians, it becomes energy of higher consciousness.

Herne's energy has the same worldview shifting pattern and power that, as Kafka put it, "shatters the frozen sea within us." The "frozen sea" alludes to the old paradigm of a disconnected universe where everything is separated. In readings, Herne also may point to other disabling beliefs holding you or someone close to you back. Herne constantly challenges old paradigms and disabling beliefs.

He and his Wild Hunt horde ride herd over your consciousness to stiffen up your courage and manifest the necessary willpower to overcome obstacles. As Holly noted, Herne's energy in a reading has a softer side. Herne is a paternal, gentle soul who helps you around invisible turns on darkened roads.

Let's travel back to Orion's Belt, which is depicted in Herne's art above his sword. Herne the Hunter has had many manifestations in mythology and folklore. He is the northern version of Orion the Hunter, who was Osiris to the Ancient Egyptians. In Ancient Egypt, Orion's Belt symbolized fraternal communication (resonance) between the seen and unseen worlds.

In a reading, Herne affords access to wise and ancient energy. His primary message is: don't procrastinate. Worldviews are shifting. Beliefs are changing. You too are changing. Allow Herne to shine the light of the wintery forest and Orion's Belt upon your dreams. In Homer's *Odyssey*, the blind prophet Tiresias promised Odysseus that the "brightest star in Orion's Belt" would guide him home on his journey. Herne the Hunter makes this same promise to you.

Reality has been described as a dream with rules. Herne reminds us that those rules are also changing.

8 – MA'AT

Painting Ma'at was a delightful task! I must confess as a young child I was completely and utterly captivated by the Ancient Egyptians and their art. There is a photograph of me at age four fast asleep on the floor with my beloved Egyptian books lying open and strewn all about me. My father often took me in hand to the Metropolitan Museum of Art in Manhattan where we would spend the day reveling in the Egyptian treasures. It was with that passion and dedication in mind that I set to painting Ma'at. I added a pond scene below her feet that features a fragment of a wall painting from the tomb of Nebamun in Thebes that I always loved. I also loved that Ma'at's wings symbolized motherly protection and that she stood for truth, order and balance, but also that she was personified as a goddess who regulated the stars.

Ma'at is the Egyptian goddess of justice and balance. The lioness goddess pictured on the card is Sekhmet, her protector. Together they symbolize the Divine Feminine and point to a lack of justice and balance that characterized many periods of human history while the Divine Feminine lived in exile. Since humanity exiled her, it is we who pay the price of imbalance and injustice in today's world.

The Egyptian civilization lasted for well over 2,500 years, and perhaps much longer. As the centers of devotion shifted between Upper and Lower Egypt, the attributes of Egyptian gods and goddesses also shifted. They became conflated with one another or saw their attributes absorbed by other deities. Egyptian culture flourished, in part, because their gods and goddesses were not immutable.

Inspired by friends, and probably the Spirit of Ma'at herself, Holly included Sekhmet in the card's symbolism. As protector, Sekhmet was known as "The one who Loves Ma'at and detests evil." She represents the feminine qualities of mercy and compassion—the last hopes of our patriarchal world.

The symbolism of the painting from Nebamun's tomb in Thebes (Luxor) adds subtle texture to Ma'at's tableau. Nebamun was a lowly grain counter unlikely even to have been known to the Pharaoh. Yet the art from his tomb ranks among the most exquisite surviving Ancient Egyptian art. The painter is not known but is referred to as "The Michelangelo of the Nile."

The surviving panels, hacked away by grave robbers, foreshadow a balanced world where neither masculine nor feminine archetypes dominate. An end to patriarchy does not presage matriarchy, but rather a return to balance. The paradisiacal pond is full of birds and fish and surrounded by gardens of lush foliage, flowers, shade trees and fruit trees—all symbols of a balanced world.

In readings, this artistic celebration of life promises a return to balance and justice and invokes the Divine Feminine protection of Ma'at and Sekhmet as we strive to create this new reality together.

9 – THE STORYTELLER

The Storyteller is an amazing card with many tales to tell. At the time I was painting the Chrysalis cards, my beloved father died at 89 and my mother moved into my home to live out her remaining years. When I began the sketches for Storyteller my mother seemed the perfect muse. She had always been such a strong woman, dedicated to her family, friends, animals, garden, as well as to her artistic endeavors. It seemed there was always brightness about her. Perhaps it was her aura, which through my hands, became Storyteller's healing orb. The thistles around Storyteller had their origins in my childhood too. My mother would create hedgehog dolls with thistle heads. The oriole that serves as the Storyteller's totem came to Toney as it perched outside his window as if asking to be included. On that note, I'd like to say how delightful this whole process was because Toney and I worked through all the cards with our eyes and ears open to signs and synchronicity at every turn!

The teasel, the orioles, the multipurpose energy orb—Storyteller's tableau is a veritable feast of magical symbolism and healing energy.

The teasel thistles rising up around Storyteller symbolize nature's verdant protection for those in need of healing. The orioles and oriole feathers inform us Storyteller is a shamanka, a self-transforming shapeshifter. The energy orb assures us Storyteller transforms and manipulates energy, the secret of her healing power.

Shapeshifting does not necessarily imply that a shamanka transforms into an animal by altering her physical appearance. It implies that shamans transform the energy present in their environment by shifting their states of consciousness and altering their energy signatures. In this way, they become vessels for healing energy.

Whenever we alter our energy signature through meditation, selfless acts, chakra work, yoga, reiki, etc., we are, in effect, utilizing our own innate shapeshifting ability. Shamans like Storyteller on the other hand accomplish this at the highest level of consciousness. Shamans become entrained or synchronized with their environment and are able to direct and manipulate pranic energy by sheer force of will. Storyteller's *Stars of Venus* in her art are two meditation mandalas to help you achieve a meditative state of consciousness.

In your reading, Storyteller and her healing orb present a nurturing, feminine presence. She uses the orb for healing and for contacting spirits, including the ancestors. Storyteller reminds you to honor the ancestors. She teaches you to remain balanced by shifting energy from the masculine Cronus to feminine Mythos and living life on the edges of time.

Storyteller is a good shamanka because she is humble. Shamans in all cultures and all those who follow the shaman's path live life selflessly in the service of others. When Storyteller appears in readings she reminds you to let go of the Ego Self to follow the shaman's path to Authentic Self.

10 – WHEEL

Most evenings as I journeyed home in Stowe, Vermont, I passed an old rambling farmhouse from the 1800's. Out front, propped against a gnarled oak tree, someone had placed an old wagon wheel. I idly watched the wagon wheel over time and through all seasons. There it stood, still and firm, decorated with wild grass and vines in summertime; rustling brown, red and gold leaves in autumn; crocus, violets and tender grass in spring, and finally draped in drifting snow and long, lovely icicles during winter. So when it came time to paint the Major Arcana for Chrysalis, my mind returned immediately to the old wagon wheel and its determined stand against the elements. It seemed the perfect wheel for our deck both in meaning and appearance. I included a lovely smudging pot of incense and an ancient goddess figure to set the stage.

L ike Storyteller's orb the wheel is a symbol of many things. The wheel of fortune stands for the fickleness called fate that seems to randomly twist between good fortune and misfortune. The goddess figurine Holly included on the Wheel's tableau could be Fortuna, the Roman goddess of fortune and good luck who dispensed fate from her wheeled throne. Or she could be Nemetona, the Celtic goddess of sacred space. Wheels, useful for spiritual teaching, were customarily located in a sacred space.

The Wheel can symbolize the Wheel of the Year, like the old wagon wheel that provided Holly's inspiration. The Celtic Wheel of the Year reminds us of the endless cycle of birth, death and rebirth. The four sacred Celtic festivals of Imbolc, Beltane, Lammas and Samhain made sure the symbolism of the wheel was honored in everyday life.

In Chrysalis, death and rebirth are rites of passage occurring in different dimensions simultaneously; you depart one dimension and seamlessly arrive in another. There is no such thing as death, per se; death is a transit between living dimensions.

The Wheel also symbolizes a Medicine Wheel, important to indigenous peoples for rituals, healings and spiritual instruction. Medicine Wheels are formed by setting out rocks arranged in a sacred or magic circle. The qualities of a magic circle are similar to those of a mandala. All paths lead to the center and represent the wholeness of Self and the universe within.

In a reading, Wheel confers the consolation of knowing everything is unfolding just as it should and that nothing is left to chance. The universe is in no hurry; seasons come and go. The message of the Wheel is to be mindful of the many cycles and patterns in your life and reflect upon their meaning and unseen origins. By doing so, you raise vague patterns in the unconscious mind into the clarity of consciousness.

11 – PAPA LEGBA

*P*apa was one of my very favorite and most mischievous subjects. When I learned Papa was to be our strength card, I became very excited. Voodoo has a long history of helping its believers achieve personal goals. Papa holds the key to the gateway between the spiritual and physical realms; the telephone poles in the distance symbolize the ease of communication between these realms. In searching for a male model for Papa, I found a fabulous photograph of a Haitian grandfather. I wanted Papa to appear accessible and yet mysterious. My mind was filled with visions of crossroads, veves, and altars burgeoning with colorful figures; of flickering candles and rhythmic ceremonies beneath the tropical moon. Soon after I sketched him, I received a request to have our Papa Legba art featured on television's 'The Auction Kings.' It seemed Papa was already acting as an intermediary for Chrysalis. I must add that while I painted Papa my daughter Esme chanted, "Happy Voodoo Gris Gris," the title of one of my books. I think Papa's spirit was in the air!

We might even say Papa's spirit and energy pervades Chrysalis Tarot! As we discussed in Chapter 2, *Papa Legba's Unseen Travels*, Chrysalis is a dialog with the Collective Unconscious. Papa, a gatekeeper and messenger, is at your side in every reading. He is our liminal, betwixt and between archetype who attends the crossroads that lead from this world to the magical world beyond. He vivifies the dialog between tarot reader, the individual cards, and the Otherworld.

Information in the form of subtle energy is transmitted from the Otherworld, a dimension that includes the Collective Unconscious, the Fairy Realm and the Ancestral Realm, and is received by the personal unconscious mind. Once there, it is processed and amplified. It then finds its way into conscious awareness through the portals of intuition, active imagination, synchronicity, lucid dreams, recollection, infused knowledge, or what we refer to as *sixth sense*.

One of the objectives of Chrysalis is to assist in sharpening your natural intuitive and psychic abilities through spiritual growth and development. All the answers, it is said, are already inside you. Tarot is a tool to tease those answers from the unconscious mind.

Papa's telephone lines accommodate two-way communication. We transmit information to the Otherworld and the Otherworld transmits information back to us in a feedforward-feedback loop. This is the way we come to know Collective Unconscious archetypes and they come to know us.

The drawing on Papa Legba's rock wall is called a *veve*. It's his Otherworld phone number, so to speak. One of the easiest ways to read Chrysalis is to take Papa from the deck and set him to one side as you perform a reading using two or three drawn cards. In no time at all you'll notice an exponential increase in your ability to understand Chrysalis cards intuitively. They are very talkative and practice makes perfect.

12 – CELTIC OWL

There's a dirt road in Stowe, Vermont, called Covered Bridge Road. 'Emily's Bridge' stands at the end of the road and has a reputation for being haunted. It was there I first saw an owl take flight right over my head. I heard a soft, swooping noise just above and realized an owl had flown over. It was a majestic and memorable sighting. When it came to painting the Celtic Owl I thought of that owl on that cold winter night. I saw it only once more in the same spot some months later. Eventually, I found a wonderful picture of a barn owl taken by nature photographer John Hendrickson. Mr. Hendrickson gave us permission to use his photo for inspiration, so our Celtic 'barn' owl was born and took flight in Chrysalis.

The owl is one of the oldest archetypes to symbolize the mysterious realm known as the Collective Unconscious. In Greek mythology, Athena was often accompanied by her *familiar,* the owl. A familiar is a totem or spirit animal.

Celtic Owl shares many attributes with Athena, who was patroness of the city of Athens. They both symbolize wisdom, courage and inspiration. Since owls see extremely well in the night, they frequently are associated with deep wisdom and the unseen world. In ancient times, individuals who were able to understand the language of the birds were regarded as seers or prophets. Owl is truly a spirit animal with special natural and supernatural powers.

The interwoven Celtic design in Holly's art symbolizes the connectivity between the seen and unseen worlds, which is thematic of Chrysalis. Indeed, this symbolism is carried forward and appears again on Celtic Owl's crown chakra, where it represents the ability to see and understand what others might fail to grasp.

The Crown or seventh chakra is the wellspring of spiritual understanding and intuition. Pranic energy enters the body at the crown chakra and flows from there through the lower six energy meridians before returning to the universal web of life.

Celtic Owl's Otherworldly essence is repeated several times in Chrysalis. Owls are featured on the Watcher, where he again appears as a familiar. On the Three of Stones, owls perch at the underground entrance to a dream chamber. Owls represent interconnectedness, personal courage and spiritual growth.

If Celtic Owl or other Chrysalis owls appear frequently in your readings, it's quite possible they are announcing themselves as your spirit animal. If true, that's wonderful news to receive. Owls indicate you can see beneath the surface of things and are quick to arrive at the heart of the matter when making decisions. Developing psychic and clairvoyant skills requires patience, practice and frequent contemplation. With Celtic Owl riding on your shoulder, these are easily learned lessons.

13 – ARIADNE

Whenever I thought of Ariadne and her labyrinth, I couldn't help but envision the labyrinth outside St. Francis Church in Santa Fe, New Mexico. I have patiently walked its circular maze many times and can only imagine the difficulty had it had actual walls. I decided to portray Ariadne in the center of the image, making her an accessible ally for transformation. Having lost both my parents during the creation of Chrysalis, Ariadne reminded me that help is always being offered in various forms and you only need seek it out. The disc and ball of yarn Ariadne holds are symbols of her assistance. Our Minotaur appears on a disc rather than in the flesh as we preferred that approach. As for Ariadne, I wanted her to be an ethereal, ethnic beauty as befits a goddess. I chose to work from photos of a Greek friend of mine. I drew two sketches of Ariadne and the second one which is pictured above won out.

The story of Ariadne's assistance is told in the myth of Ariadne's Thread. Her lover, Theseus, journeyed to the center of the labyrinth to do battle with the dreaded half-man, half-bull called a Minotaur. To make certain he could trace his way out, Ariadne gave Theseus the end of a ball of yarn she used in weaving—all Great Mother goddesses are weavers.

Traversing the labyrinth is a metaphor for self-discovery, self-emptying and shadow work. In the labyrinth's sacred center we battle things we don't much like about who we are—things we hide from ourselves. The battle with the shadow self teaches us how to forgive and love who we are and how to bring our demons out of hiding.

We enter the labyrinth's maze with confused emotions and submerged guilt and later emerge whole, balanced and with greater self-confidence. The spiraling labyrinth symbolizes the energy of the Hero's Journey using Chrysalis Tarot. It is a spiritual exercise involving peaceful mindfulness and rigorous self-examination.

Slaying the Minotaur shines light upon the fearful shadowy projections that haunt your psyche and teaches you to live fully in the present moment.

In your reading, Ariadne invites you to take note of, and assume responsibility for, any unhealthy attitudes and attachments that may constrain emotional and intellectual freedom. By slaying your dreaded Minotaur, you reclaim all power it held over you—the fear-based power that you yourself unwittingly allowed the Minotaur to steal.

Ariadne and the Minotaur symbolize the heroic battle to overcome fear, the scourge of spiritual fulfillment and joy of living. As a reward for slaying the Minotaur, the Minoan Mother Goddess Ariadne promises threads of divine assistance and loving protection in all your future endeavors.

14 – GOLDEN FLOWER

*A*s an artist I have always wanted to try my hand at painting a rather large mandala. But thus far the Golden Flower is the only one I've created. Still, the seeds are planted. The most perplexing bit of it all was where to put my signature and not interrupt the flow. I think a mandala is the perfect illustration for temperance, harmony and meditation. As Longchenpa said, "A mandala is an integrated structure organized around a unifying center." *When it came to adding the visual elements, I settled upon the fish from my astrological sign, Pisces. Perhaps it's only my little secret, but I feel one of Pisces' strong suits is an ability to see and understand circumstances and different opinions from both sides of the fence. Such compassionate thinking seemed a necessity for a contemplative card such as the Golden Flower.*

Each of the two urns or vases in Holly's Golden Flower art contains a genie. We'll come back to the two genies in a moment.

C.G. Jung's writings about the Golden Flower inspired our inclusion of this concept within our Major Arcana cards. Jung often lamented the triumph of Western intellectualism (science and scholarship) over Eastern mysticism (meditation and wisdom), particularly the mystical practices of Chinese Taoists.

As Holly noted, Golden Flower is a mandala—a magic circle or wheel. During Taoist meditation, the mandala is imagined as a gently rotating orb centered between the eyes. The Golden Flower meditation technique is simple: 1) you sit erect so you won't impede your breathing or the natural flow of pranic energy; 2) you contemplate in silence as you allow thoughts to swim by freely like the fish in the art. The rewards over time are great. You will notice increased energy, perception and awareness.

"Only after one hundred days of consistent work, only then is the light genuine; only then can one begin to work with the spirit-fire," according to an ancient Taoist text. The "spirit-fire" refers to Seeds of Self that meditation nurtures to spiritual maturity. Spirit-fire penetrates the seeds and develops them rhythmically as the wheel turns slowly during meditation.

The butterflies symbolize meditative consciousness. They express spiritual empowerment as they flee hindering leaves of the intellect. Their flight symbolizes what Chrysalis calls *transpersonal soul making*, the lighter-than-air meditative awareness that transcends Self.

In readings, the Golden Flower symbolizes drawing closer to higher consciousness through meditation or contemplation. Salvaging core values and re-balancing life's priorities empower you to free the spirit-fire genies within. Your two genies will reappear frolicking in the Tree of Life as two fairies on the Nine of Mirrors card, a Chrysalis personal empowerment card.

15 – BELLA ROSA

*B*ella Rosa is a Venetian muse who epitomizes the spirit of the Carnival of Venice. Our mysterious, androgynous free spirit holds court during the renowned annual masquerade ball. During the time I painted Bella Rosa, my dear friend Mariana in Romania sent me an amazing series of photographs of the costumes at the Carnival. I was hard-pressed to settle on a costume, there were so many utterly gorgeous ones. I felt Toney's idea of depicting tarot's traditional devil as a costumed Venetian at the Carnival was pure genius. There is an endlessly enigmatic aspect to a masked individual. I chose to remove any hint of humanity behind the mask by making the eyes empty, cavernous black holes. This shadowy quality leaves interpretation to the viewer's imagination.

As Holly noted, Bella Rosa is enigmatic because we hide so many characteristics of our true nature from the outside world. The masks we wear—the false personas—can become problematic over time. This is Bella's primary message: unresolved issues will prevent us from being comfortable in our own skin.

We don't know much about Bella. He or she easily could be a lauded member of Venetian nobility or one of their lowly servants. That was the beauty of the annual masked ball—you could be anyone you wished! For most of us that's fun for a little while, but one can't, or at least shouldn't, go through life habitually being untrue to their nature, lest a false persona rise up and assert dominance.

Owning dark issues lodged in the shadow is crucial to spiritual and physical well-being. We all have a dark side; it's a part of human nature. Most of us manage to get on with a well managed small-scale Jekyll and Hyde duality. But to attain enlightenment, we must recognize and integrate into conscious awareness darker aspects of who we really are.

Self-acceptance begins by accepting our dark side and dredging up dross—the rotting pain and poison of unforgiveness, regret and internalized conflict. When we learn how to forgive and embrace ourselves we can sustain positive relationships.

Once the shadow is integrated, we automatically will stop projecting its dark side onto other people, since there's no longer a valid reason to deny its existence. Bella's red rose symbolizes self-acceptance. The mirror symbolizes introspection—the shining light that exposes the shadow's favorite hiding places.

Jung wrote, *"One does not become enlightened by imagining figures of light, but by making the darkness conscious."* The infinity shaped ouroboros is a serpent that continually consumes its tail. The serpent's role through time immemorial has been to awaken humanity from its slumbering darkness and illuminate pathways to enlightenment.

16 – KALI

Though I painted this Kali card, the image is disturbing to me. I had never attempted anything 'dark' before. But it's one of the few paintings where I felt the piece painted itself, rather like the ill-fated portrait in Oscar Wilde's Picture of Dorian Gray. *The many paintings I reviewed before beginning Kali portrayed her fearful and ferocious Mother Goddess form. Her destructive yet creative cleansing energy was evident in those Hindu paintings, but I also observed a light quality as well. Perhaps it was the stylized, colorful approach of the Indian works that lighten her essence, but it seems my Kali took on a darker persona. All things considered, I think the Dark Mother makes a very strong visual statement. To me that's what this card's message is all about. Kali wants you to sit up and take notice much like Dorian Gray's portrait. Beauty and order are restored in the end!*

Archetypes that symbolize creative destruction are essential to the Hero's Journey and should be recognized. Chrysalis has two: Kali and Phoenix. While Kali's solutions are mostly impersonal, imposed and often resisted, Phoenix's solutions represent voluntary acts of personal sacrifice that are readily accepted.

Accordingly, when we see Kali in a reading we might anticipate a far reaching, large-scale consequence. Or, we might take it as an urgent tap on the shoulder to call attention to some neglected situation. Kali asks us to accept personal responsibility for affecting needed changes in our lives, or at least to grudgingly accept them. Otherwise, she may be required to make the changes for us.

Kali's world is always a work in progress, a world of chaos and uncertainty. Although her actions have purpose, which she foresees far in advance, we lack that capacity of foresight. Kali's world is a nonlinear jigsaw puzzle seemingly carved into too many pieces. Many of them must remain hidden for our own well-being.

Kali's garland of skulls symbolizes higher consciousness. Holly added Sanskrit writing since legend has it that Kali inspired the Sanskrit alphabet. Her Third Eye reminds us to use intuition and remain open to new ways of thinking. Such openness is the key to locating the cornerpieces in Kali's crazy puzzle. Cornerpieces help you identify situations in life, e.g. people, beliefs, bad habits, etc. that become obstacles to self-fulfillment. Kali will then motivate you to act appropriately. Like a jigsaw puzzle, Kali hides her solutions in plain sight.

We tend to forget Mother Goddesses have benign and fearful aspects. Doting on benign, sentimental visions of the Divine Feminine separates her from us. We can best appreciate Kali when we can embrace the paradoxical nature of all Great Mother Goddesses: they are destroyers and creators, their actions are creative destruction.

Kali is known as the Divine Mother of the Universe. She reminds us of our divine nature and the wonders of cosmic awareness.

17 – ELPI

Elpi is the epitome of everlasting hope and faith. I myself had such high hopes for her visually, but in the end she is probably the one Chrysalis card I'd like to create anew. Even so, I've gotten wonderful feedback from people saying how much they love the Elpi image, so I guess I can finally release the urge to change her. I used to read the tarot frequently for friends and in my youth the Star was my favorite card because of its message of hope and faith. I remember loving it so much that I painted a large version of the Star card on my bedroom door. Whenever I bought a new Tarot deck, I would always look at the Star card first. I love Elpi's energy and the fact that the four cardinal winds assist her in her nightly endeavor. Symbolically, it's a beautiful card!

When we chose Elpi to be our archetype of everlasting hope, we simply personified the symbolism of tarot's Star card. Elpis— (we shortened her Greek name)—was a minor deity and sky goddess known as a daimon in the Greek pantheon. In mythology the daimones were benevolent nature spirits. All daimones in Chrysalis Tarot have dual roles as fairies led by Morgan le Fay, the Chrysalis Sorceress and Queen of Faeries.

Elpi is a queen in her own right. She is Queen of the Night and this is her story.

Zeus, who delighted in creating havoc for mortals because they stole fire, trapped all the daimones, good and bad, in a jar and trusted it to the care of the first woman who was named Pandora. He instructed Pandora not to open the jar (or box) knowing full well that curiosity would get the best of her—and it did.

When Pandora opened the box all the daimones escaped back into the abode of the gods including Elpi's counterpart, Moros, the spirit of hopelessness, depression and doom. Only Elpi remained behind to comfort mankind. "That is why Elpi (Hope) alone is still found among the people, promising that she will bestow on each of us the good things that have gone away," explained Aesop in one of his famous fables.

We converted Pandora's jar into Elpi's Golden Censor. Each evening with help from her four Anemoi steeds, Elpi whisked across the darkened sky to sprinkle stars from her golden censor. The Anemoi are gods of the four cardinal winds and sons of the planets and stars. We're perhaps most familiar with the Anemoi, Zephyrus, who controls the spring breezes and west winds. Anemoi are depicted as horses, a symbol of divine power.

Elpi's scarf is a stylized ouroboros designed by Holly especially for her. An ouroboros symbolizes the primordial cosmic unity of all things that never can be extinguished from the human heart—things such as hope.

18 - MOON

I was extremely excited about painting the Moon card. For a few years before Chrysalis came into being, I dreamed ideas and made sketches for a decorative painting of the moon. In a way, Chrysalis was the manifestation of that dream. I held fond memories of the moonlight on the hills outside our country cabin. My father would take me outside on warm summer evenings to smell the Tabac Blanc flowers. It's said the flowers of this particular plant give off their scent only at night. I remember my father insisting moonlight enhanced the experience! In Chrysalis, the crescent moon rises to illuminate a watery path in the mysterious world of the night. The moon is a feminine force, primal and ancient, symbolizing creation's darkest mysteries. In half-light she reveals the island of inspiration that poets, artists, musicians and mystics know well.

The scent of moonlight is indeed a scent of mystery and magic. The moon is the mystical abode of the Divine Feminine's cohort of Mother Goddesses. The 8-point Star of Ishtar featured prominently in the art is symbolic of the goddesses who followed Ishtar and were awarded the epithets Queen of Heaven and Star of the Sea. In addition to Ishtar, the list includes Inanna, Isis, Aphrodite, Astarte and others.

The oceans like the moon symbolize the unconscious mind, the dwelling place of waking and sleeping dreams, intuition and active imagination. Wine-dark seas glistening with moonlight have long symbolized the Great Mother and the feminine principle.

The Moon in a reading can be a life changing card. It can teach you how to listen to your inner voice, the voice of the Great Mother, and lead you to place great trust in her. Many cards in Chrysalis help develop the intuitive skills we all have. As those skills develop, so does the sixth sense of clairsentience, which is the art of feeling knowledge. Clairsentience, also a metaphysical sense we all have, is the art of knowing that something is right without knowing why, and without the need to analyze or intellectualize it. This sense is the wellspring of empathy, compassion and consolation.

In Chrysalis, clairsentience is best illustrated by the Six of Scrolls that depicts an elephant and a fairy connected to one another in deep thought. Elephants are perhaps the most clairsentient of all creatures. John Dunn called elephants, "nature's great masterpieces."

When we experience inexplicable knowing we experience Moon magic and divine inspiration—delights to be contemplated, not analyzed. In a reading, Moon may be asking you to ramp your right brain up for greater yin and yang balance and energy. Consistent work with Chrysalis will help engender such balance; the western mind, as we all know, is conditioned to be left brain oriented. That's why Chrysalis is a feminine deck inspired by the Moon's nocturnal yin energy.

19 – SUN

I am very fond of sun faces! Perhaps this is because as a young artist I spent much of my time practicing human features over and over again. Painting the sun allows a tremendous amount of decorative freedom. I discovered a wonderful book on Indian art called India: Decoration, Interiors, Design *by Henry Wilson. The background of my sun painting was inspired by a beautifully painted Indian mural featured in his book. I found Indian influence to be important when considering the sun card. In yoga, the practicing of physical poses is called Hatha yoga. In Sanskrit, Hameans (sun) and Tha (moon), joined with the word 'yoga' means to unify. Hatha yoga balances and unites the sun (male) and moon (female) energies in the body. When using Chrysalis, we unify those energies in order to become whole and achieve a peaceful spirit. When I painted the moon and sun cards, I was careful to paint them concurrently.*

The Sun is the most joyful of tarot cards and a wonderful card to have in a reading. Like all cards in Chrysalis, Sun is multivalent—it has many meanings and interpretations. The *correct* meaning is always the one your mind attributes to a card. We take from a card or a reading what the Otherworld intends with one caveat. If we attempt to analyze or rationalize the card, that itself is an act of ego rather than intuition. The resulting interpretation may be less than satisfying and nonproductive.

We mention this because the Sun is a rational *yang* card. However, we softened him with a *yin* touch—a tiny teardrop Holly placed there, not to dampen the joy or distract from Sun's vibrant optimism, but to provide another layer of meaning.

As an archetype for the god Apollo, the Sun may look down upon Earth and lament the absence of yin/yang balance Holly mentioned. He may lament the exploitation of nature and the patriarchal suppression of women, who have been closely associated with nature for eons. He may lament the abandonment of the Apollonian Ideals that the Sun represents; ideals such as beauty, truth and justice.

He naturally would lament these culture-bound imbalances since Sun is a symbol of enlightenment. In fact, enlightenment and the Apollonian Ideals are the primary source of the Sun's joy and optimism. Since Chrysalis is a holistic deck devoted to deep ecology, we would be remiss if we failed to mention that domination by worldly power is a far cry from enlightenment and a corruption of the Sun's virtue.

Sun in readings asks us to think holistically. He asks us to root our ideals in pastures of cooperation not competition, and to seek a pastoral balance of masculine and feminine energies on Earth.

20 – PHOENIX

*C*oincidentally, I was painting the Phoenix card around the time that *my daughter Esme and I enjoyed one of our 'Harry Potter' movie marathons. I found an inspirational Phoenix in JK Rowling's Fawkes. Dumbledore's quote still sticks in my mind, "Fascinating creatures, phoenixes. They can carry immensely heavy loads, their tears have healing powers, and they make highly faithful pets." The beauty of the Phoenix's amazing regenerative powers was what made him such a wonderful choice for the Chrysalis line up. Having gone through many transformations in my own life, I know the very act of transformation is strengthening. I keep a little illustration of a Phoenix in the corner of my bedroom mirror to remind me I always have the ability to recreate myself, even if from only a pile of ashes. I think Phoenix symbolizes worthy advice to pass on to our youth: it's always possible, no matter how hopeless one feels, to rise again!*

The Phoenix appears at the point in the Hero's Journey when only a little work remains. The time has come for the archetypal act of self-judgment. You have forgiven yourself, your parents, and anyone else in need of your forgiveness. This doesn't mean that whatever transgressions were committed against you are suddenly okay. It only means that you're prepared to set yourself free and move on.

You performed difficult shadow work. You now can acknowledge your dark side and admit your human imperfections. Rather than project these imperfections onto others, you integrated them into your psyche. It is no longer fractured or shattered but whole. You accepted yourself as you are. You are self-empowered.

The Hero's Journey requires such hard work. It's more than simply talking the talk. It's breaking free of cultural and religious chains that kept you bound and anguished in the fires of infirmity. When the time arrived to judge yourself worthy and take flight from the smoldering ashes of brokenness, you responded. The time has now arrived to rise up in grace, glory and splendor.

If the Phoenix appears in the early stages of your Hero's Journey, she points to the work at hand: the transformation of consciousness through communication with your archetypal spirit guides and your ancestors who live eternally. They are immortal just as you are immortal. The Phoenix symbolizes a time of resolution and restoration on your journey.

Phoenix is the ageless sacred firebird, the primordial and multicultural symbol of immortality. She is the penultimate symbol of the Authentic Self in Chrysalis Tarot.

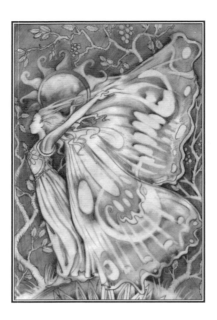

21 - PSYCHE

The idea for Psyche's painting existed long before any of the Chrysalis cards were even a sparkle in their creators' eyes. When Toney and I decided Psyche should play a starring role in our lineup, I immediately reflected upon a 'Butterfly Woman' image I'd put aside to save. After some research into the Greek Goddess of the Soul, I was delighted to find that my image would serve Psyche magnificently. I stumbled across so many amazing synchronicities! One example is the story of "Cupid and Psyche" from the Latin novel Metamorphoses. *I also found a Roman mosaic depicting Psyche with butterfly wings. And finally, during a hike in Sedona I spotted a woman atop a local rock formation with large butterfly wings attached to her arms. How cleverly it all fit together. I began to feel that Psyche with her hopeful message that metamorphosis is always possible is truly the essence of Chrysalis!*

Since the word *psyche* in Greek means butterfly or *soul*, Holly and I agreed that Psyche was a perfect fit for the final card in Chrysalis' Major Arcana. She represents transformation of the soul, spiritual ascension and personal enlightenment. Psyche and the butterfly personify the ultimate reward of the Hero's Journey: the emergence from the chrysalis of Authentic Self, the soul's highest calling.

In readings, Psyche tells us to mind the thresholds; it's easy to become stuck in one. Life is about growth and change. Being stuck in a threshold is a metaphor for listening to some other voice rather than to your heart. With so much new knowledge being discovered daily, one needs to get used to holding contradictory ideas in the mind simultaneously. Refusing to grow by examining one's beliefs is to cling to the security of the threshold and go nowhere.

The cards in Chrysalis Tarot are designed to assist getting across sticky thresholds. Best to be like the merry lady dancing on the summit of Bell rock. She was celebrating the breathtaking discovery of a higher perspective, the type of discovery that makes crossing thresholds an everyday matter.

When Psyche appears in a reading, you may see yourself looking up from the base of Bell rock rather than merrily dancing on top of it. If so, Psyche calls you to surrender your heart to her and her cohort of archetypes, spirit guides, fairies, shamans and spirit animals. Surrender—the act of letting go—is the first lesson of rock climbing in Chrysalis Tarot. The act of self-emptying is the second.

MINOR ARCANA CARDS

A tarot reading is like a gestalt—the whole of the reading is greater than the sum of its parts. These are the 40 cards in the Minor Arcana; 40 parts that provide mortar to hold your reading together and illuminate its meaning.

Chrysalis Minor Arcana cards are helpers that could be called the hands of the Major Arcana archetypes. They help you make wise choices and heal by helping you know yourself better and become more introspective. They help you with shadow work, which integrates things we prefer to hide from ourselves and from others—the things we dislike about ourselves and our past—into conscious awareness.

They help you celebrate achievements and place expectations that fell short of the mark into proper perspective nonjudgmentally. They help you engender synchronicity, the mystical language of the archetypes. Synchronous moments are magical moments that assure you that you never walk alone.

Chrysalis Minor Arcana cards have special qualities that illuminate the road to destiny. One is the quality of being polysemous—there are many meanings and interpretations to Chrysalis cards. The interpretations offered here are merely lanterns to keep you from becoming overwhelmed by information. As you get to know the cards, and they get to know you, the lanterns become brighter and magnified by the lens of your intuition.

The Minor Arcana cards are divided into four suits:

STONES, MIRRORS, SPIRALS and SCROLLS

These suits correspond respectively to Earth, Water, Fire and Air.

STONES
represent the material
world (Earth).

MIRRORS
represent feelings and
emotions (Water).

SPIRALS
represent energy
and spirit (Fire).

SCROLLS
represent the intellect
and intuition (Air).

ACE OF STONES

The original sketch for the Ace of Stones varies greatly from the painting we now see. I feel very strongly about the aces because they set the stage atmospherically for the rest of their suit. So, in the end I settled on a standing stone with dawn breaking in the sky behind it to usher in the Suit of Stones. It's one of my favorite cards visually and a recent occurrence made it all the more interesting. On a visit to a metaphysical shop in Sedona, I talked with the owner about carrying Chrysalis Tarot. As we thumbed through the cards, she happened upon the Ace of Stones and exclaimed, "Do you realize what you have painted here?" *I replied,* "Yes, a standing stone." *She said,* "No, you have painted Auralite-23, a 1.2 billon-year-old stone formed around the time of the first multi-celluar creatures." *It seems our Ace of Stones has quite a history!*

Our entire Suit of Stones was inspired by the earth energies in the UK's West Country, home to the Arthurian legends, stone circles, countless megalithic monuments like our Ace of Stones, and other mysteries embedded deep in the energy grids that crisscross the Mystical Isles like a spider web. When you walk across these grids, called ley lines, you can sense the energy.

The earth energy beneath standing stones, stone circles, holy wells and other monuments have qualities similar to crystals. Energy healing accomplished with crystals, earth energy, tarot, shamanic energy and other healing modalities resonate with and unblock the body's seven energy-meridian chakras. Auralite-23 crystals, like those in the Ace of Stones, contain minerals associated with unblocking or clearing all seven chakras.

Auralite-23 is known as the *Paradigm Shifter*. Holly and I knew nothing of Auralite-23 when we conceived the Suit of Stones and the Ace of Stones was sketched. This ace is a monument to the synchronicity generated by Chrysalis, which itself is designed to herald a paradigm shift.

The chakras are portals to your eternal Higher Self. They radiate energy that draws you toward transformation and your personal destiny. Many use this ace as a grounding card and keep it on the bottom of the Chrysalis deck when it's not in use. The chakras also unlock spiritual gifts such as clairsentience and clairvoyance, the highest forms of Third Eye intuition.

Other Chrysalis Minor Arcana cards are also intricately linked to chakra clearing. In your reading, the Ace of Stones reminds you to plan your path thoughtfully and diligently. This card marks a new beginning and a new way of perceiving the abundance of information presented by the Minor Arcana.

Of all Chrysalis archetypes, mythological figures and high-energy healing cards, few can match the healing energy or synchronicity generated by the Ace of Stones. It's always a welcome card to see in your readings.

TWO OF STONES

Around the time I painted the Two of Stones, I experienced two sightings *of bears near my home in Stowe, Vermont. These were amazing to me because I'd never seen a bear in the wild before. In the first situation, I spied a bear cub that practically skipped across the road in front of me. The second involved a bear standing by the side of the road near a large embankment. When he heard my vehicle approaching, he leapt up and over an extremely steep rock outcropping. I was awestruck such a large animal would have such amazing dexterity! I often thought of bears when painting the Minor Arcana. When it came to the idea of visually showing trust, I will admit I was stultified for a time. Then it occurred to me that when climbing animals combine ability and trust, then their trust in that next step is solid. As a spirit animal, the bear is seen as a strong source of support in times of difficulty. It provides courage and a stable foundation to face our challenges and trust our choices.*

Cards numbered two in tarot are about maintaining balance and making patient, well-discerned choices. This idea is perfectly symbolized by the bear that appears to be carefully considering his next step. In only a few moments time, informed instinct and intuition will likely take control and the bear will jump or retreat.

So what informs intuition? Memory, for certain, is one factor. Logic and past experience are others. The bear uses all three. In Chrysalis Tarot, we focus on another factor called synchronicity that goes hand-in-hand with intuition. A shaman, the most intuitive of humans, considers many things before making a decision: the flight path of birds, the sounds heard in nature, recognizing both patterns and disrupted patterns. All impart spiritual significance and meaning. All help avoid impulse, which more often than not will result in poor decisions.

In a reading, the bear points to instinct, intuition and impulse as you consider your next step. This bear has emerged from hibernation. You can almost hear the frozen ice crackle in protest to the springtime sun. Hibernation symbolizes the unconscious mind and introspection.

The bear invites you to pay close attention to your surroundings for tell-tale signs of synchronicity. Allow these signs to confirm your thoughts and influence your decisions. And by all means, opt for patience and resist acting impulsively. That's a deep ravine the bear must cross.

THREE OF STONES

I've seen some old 19th century photographs of the entryway to New-grange in Ireland. The view, before its excavation and restoration, served as inspiration for the Three of Stones. I loved that in the old photographs one catches only a glimpse of the wonders beyond the famous Newgrange carved stone. In fact, the tomb's entrance is almost hidden by wild grass, ivy, bracken and fallen stones. The dark opening seems to beckon the viewer forward. Newgrange, which was constructed around 3200 BC, is among the oldest surviving buildings in the world. I felt quite satisfied with my sketch until it came time to paint the image. It then occurred to me to add an animal or two. I decided on a council of wise owls perched about a campfire to fill the empty foreground. When I did this, I felt much more satisfied with the piece. As a 'spirit animal' the owl is characteristic of a deep connection with wisdom and intuitive knowledge, so they made the perfect planning team.

The entranceway to the underground chamber in our Three of Stones, like the entranceway to ancient Newgrange, is a trilithon arrangement—a large rock slab situated across the top of two equally large standing stones called megaliths. And similar to Newgrange, this entranceway beckons you forward into a darkened passageway beneath the Tree of Life.

It's up to your imagination to decide how you wish to use this mysterious chamber. In Cornwall, UK, it likely would mark the entrance to a *fogou*, a dream chamber once used by a Celtic shaman. The entrance pictured on the Three of Stones is also a personal passageway to the dream world. The Three of Stones encourages you to explore the depths of the Collective Unconscious, the memory bank of humankind. In the Otherworld of the Collective Unconscious, you tease out answers already inside you.

These wise, protective owls tell you that it's time to move forward; cards numbered three in tarot point to advancement. Moving forward, however, requires firm trust and confidence in the Unseen Realm. This is true whether the Unseen speaks to you through dreams, meditation or when journeying in the solitude of a darkened chamber.

The three triquetra designs symbolize the Tree of Life's interconnectedness to all things. In Norse mythology, three Norns lived beneath the Tree of Life. They were named Past, Present and Future, which are also the names of our three owls. The reason for these names is because there is no separation of time where the stuff of dreams is created. Past, present and future dissolve into the eternal now.

The Three of Stones symbolizes an important step forward toward enlightenment. Allow the owl's inner light and keen foresight to guide you.

FOUR OF STONES

For a very long time I hung onto a beautiful photograph of a pathway into a jungle. There was a manmade archway over the path and much of the stonework was covered with moss. The picture had a strong Asian feel to it, and I found it quite intriguing. When it came to drawing ideas for the Four of Stones this pathway came to mind. I then went on the hunt for elaborate, decorative trunks and chests. The one I finally settled on was Celtic in style, so I decided it might be fun to combine the two images. I feel I succeeded in altering the Asian feel and making it Celtic. I wanted the chest to remain closed as a reminder that we don't often look at or use our possessions but cling to them nonetheless. Sometimes they become burdens that follow us about or block our way towards thoughtful organization and new possibilities. I decided to depict the four stones as jeweled embellishments on the chest glimmering, so alluring, and yet at the same time restricting.

Possessions certainly can restrict or forestall the personal quest for higher matters in life, which also are bejeweled, sparkling and alluring. But there's no reason why we can't possess both. They are not mutually exclusive. As with many things in life, balance is key. The Four of Stones is one of those Chrysalis cards that ask you to be honest with yourself about your long-term goals.

Cards numbered four in tarot focus attention on stability and structure. The chest that temporarily blocks an ascending path into the jungle of uncertainty symbolizes the stability of financial security and the structure of established priorities. The archway symbolizes the choice between something old (whatever is squirreled away in the treasure chest) and something new and mysterious that lies in the great beyond.

Like the dream chamber entrance to the Three of Stones, the archway itself is a sure sign of something new. While beckoning you forward it assures you that whatever waits on the other side will fill a thousand treasure chests. It assures you that you'll find this chest with its glimmering and sparkling allure right where you left it when you return.

The Four of Stones in a reading cautions you against overvaluing worldly things you stow away in a treasure chest. The higher matters in life are also to be treasured. This card also cautions against fabricating false choices—both the material and spiritual matters in life are to be savored.

FIVE OF STONES

When I contemplated how to depict desolation, a few of my own 'dark nights of the soul' came to mind. I can recall one in particular that occurred many years ago in Hong Kong. The details don't matter as much as the emotions and sensations I experienced during the ordeal. There was a sense of aloneness and a tendency to retreat further into myself. This retreat is what I hoped to portray with my grieving figure. When I contemplated the setting, I began to think about the standing stones I'd seen in the British Isles. I always felt they had an air of grieving about them, standing like stark reminders of people and places lost to the ages. In any case, if we make it through dark times and shed that which weighed us down, then we will open up once again even wider than before. This can happen many times over on our spiritual journey.

This card introduces two aspects of healing energy in Chrysalis Tarot, that of fairies, the Gentle Folk, and that of trees, the children of Gaia. Let's talk about trees first. The one pictured could be a wild cherry tree symbolizing regeneration, or a rowan tree symbolizing the healing energy of fairies. Both species produce beautiful red berries. Wild cherry trees are among the first trees to sprout in a forest desolated by fire. Rowans, known as mountain ash trees, have long been associated with fairies and healing.

Cards numbered five in tarot often point to dark-cloud challenges. In a reading both the rowan and wild cherry tree point to its silver lining—a trial that must be endured, perhaps, or a lesson that must be learned. The fairy appears on the Five of Stones as a loving symbol of healing and the hope of brighter days. Fairy energy is an example of a coherent energy pattern that Chrysalis users learn to perceive with experience. Other examples include spirit animals, guardian spirits and, of course, the archetypes.

This particular fairy is known as a dryad, a nature spirit that protects trees. If we pay close attention to the symbols, we note the spirals on her dress (energy of change), her fairy wings (spiritual energy of healing) and the wild cherry or rowan tree (energy of regeneration). On this card, we can intuit components of the energy of catharsis—healing through the healthy release of built up fear, guilt or resentment.

The magical element to catharsis is often overlooked. It's the energy of gratitude and appreciation. As Holly noted, if we shed whatever weighs us down by choosing to focus instead on the things we have to be grateful for, we raise our vibration to cloudy heights of silver linings. Gratitude in the face of desolation demonstrates a power to bring about catharsis and change circumstances. In other words, gratitude holds the power to heal.

SIX OF STONES

This card provided me with an opportunity to use one of my favorite motifs, the Tree of Life, and in this case a Celtic Tree of Life. Some years before painting Chrysalis, my girls gifted me with a large decorative Celtic tapestry. The central focus is a stylized tree painted in a circle as if it were a Celtic knot. The Tree of Life is a common symbol in world mythologies and philosophies, so it seemed fitting for Chrysalis' multicultural philosophy. It seemed natural to use Celtic knots in lieu of bark. The patterning was to symbolize the flow of personal growth from the roots to the tips of the branches. Since this card's meaning is 'caritas', I thought it appropriate to have the gemstones hang from the limbs, as if the tree itself was offering its shimmering fruit as gifts to the world.

Holly designed the perfect tableau for *caritas*, a Latin term for the unconditional love known as charity. Cards numbered six in tarot imply the reconciliation or integration of opposites, as well as the restoration of balance and harmony. The opposites in the Six of Stones are the fruits borne by *giving and receiving*.

The gold colored stones are known as heliodors, the "gifts of the sun;" the green stones are emeralds symbolizing the vitality of the human heart and caritas, the "gift of giving." Both gemstones are a type of beryl, a talisman closely associated with higher consciousness and healing.

Heliodors connect to the energy of the third chakra at the solar plexus. This is the chakra of our natural gifts, the gifts of self-esteem, willpower and inner-knowing. The third chakra is unblocked by *receiving* the healing energy of the heliodors.

Emeralds connect to the energy of the fourth or heart chakra. This is the chakra of selflessness, charity and the Higher Self. The fourth chakra is unblocked by *giving* the healing energy of compassion through acts of loving kindness to others.

In the Tree of Life these two forms of pranic energy flow from the universe to the tree's branches and down to the roots through the trunk and then out again. With us prana flows from the universe to the crown chakra, down through the heart and solar plexus and then returns to the universal source. This nature of giving and receiving pranic energy is karmic—the more we give the more we receive and the more we grow in spiritual awareness.

In a reading, the Six of Stones draws attention to healing through giving, and to charity, self-acceptance and the acceptance of others. It may also spark an interest in chakra clearing and alignment. Prana should flow freely through each of us just as it does through the Celtic Tree of Life.

SEVEN OF STONES

I first completed this sketch with a satyr seated in front of the arched stones. I thought he made the perfect melancholy figure, illustrative of regret. When it came time to paint the piece I felt dissatisfied with his pose. I decided to ask my younger daughter Esme to pose for me. In order to get the proper angle, I had her sit and attempt a rather despondent pose at the base of a staircase. That way I could look down at her. Utilizing this sketch of Esme, I placed her amongst the river reeds with the seven-stone arch above her head. In Greek mythology Syrinx was a beautiful and chaste nymph. When she was hounded by the amorous Pan, she ran to the river's edge to ask for help from the river nymphs. To save her, the nymphs transformed Syrinx into hollow marsh reeds that made a haunting sound when Pan's frustrated breath blew across them. There you have the origin of Pan's pipes.

The Seven of Stones is about dealing with regret and appreciating music as a means of healing. Eventually, Syrinx is able to get on with her life and toss regret in the River Ladon, pictured flowing behind the archway.

The red poppies growing on the archway symbolize the goddess Demeter, who, like Syrinx, is closely identified with the River Ladon in Greek mythology. In Demeter's case, anger and regret were the issues. She was able to let go of both by washing them away in the great river.

We generally cope with regret of past actions in one of two ways. We deny the actions were wrong, or we deny responsibility for them and blame someone else. However, neither alleviates suffering and only compounds the problem. What truly overcomes such suffering is letting go of regret altogether, just as Demeter and Syrinx did.

Cards numbered seven in tarot point to spiritual introspection and completion. We can see that Syrinx is being introspective and suffering dearly. In a reading if this card finds you, or someone you care for, in a similar situation, it may be helpful to mention that we alone can extinguish the fires of suffering and unhappiness. Syrinx is able to toss regret in the river once she shoulders the responsibility for her own happiness.

The Greek philosopher Pythagoras taught listening to music everyday improves one's physical and emotional health. He called it, "music medicine." Every organ, bone and cell in the body has its own resonant frequency. Musical intervals bring us into harmony with the frequencies of these bodily vibrations. The intervals are music medicine for the body. So in one way or another, Pan's pipes are very healing.

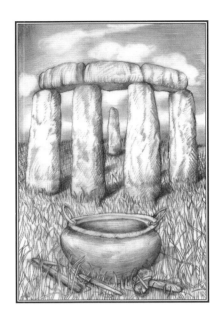

EIGHT OF STONES

I *must admit Stonehenge came immediately to mind when I first saw the keyword 'ingenuity' for the Eight of Stones. I was elated because a recent trip to England included a day trip to Amesbury where the renowned prehistoric monument is located. This was one of the few cards that didn't require very much thought; the connection with word and illustration was instantaneous. After laying out the stones in a pleasing way in the sketch, I began to think it would be wonderful to indicate some aspects of the history that had occurred there throughout the ages. I began to research ancient tools and animals. The caldron in the center implies ceremony; the pictograms imply magic and belief, and the animals imply ritual and survival. After my research, I was stumped as to how to incorporate all these items into one small painting. It then occurred to me to paint them as if they were petroglyphs in the grass.*

All megalithic monuments are grounded by earth energy. The sites on which they stand were chosen by their builders because the ground beneath was considered sacred, or because it was determined that the location was an important energy nodal on a ley line. Ley lines mark energy meridians of the Earth like chakras mark energy meridians of the body.

Many megalithic sites the world over appear to be built on ley line alignments, including Stonehenge, the Egyptian pyramids, the temples at Angkor Wat and Machu Picchu. Many researchers believe the energy at these sacred sites has a revitalizing and healing nature.

Cards numbered eight in tarot point to boundaries and opportunities. Stonehenge reminds you that self-limiting boundaries are illusions that douse the fires of opportunity and stifle the faculties of ingenuity and imagination. The self-limiting notion of boundaries was alien to the builders of Stonehenge, the pyramids and the mountaintop city of Machu Picchu.

Chrysalis cards that picture one or more megaliths (large stones) remind us of the importance of staying grounded. Working with tarot is energy work; tarot's archetypes are the organizing principles for coherent energy patterns. Being grounded, centered and balanced permits proper flow of energy throughout the body.

Meditation is one of the most effective ways to achieve grounding. Enjoying an outdoor walk in natural surroundings is another. A 10-minute nature walk goes a long way toward relieving stress and grounding chakras.

In your reading, the Eight of Stones symbolizes cosmic balance—the cycle of building up and tearing down wheeled across spans of endless time. This card reminds you to appreciate the many wonders shrouded in mystery and magic that were handed down to us by the ancients. With ingenuity and imagination we can hope one day to appreciate the many secrets they contain.

NINE OF STONES

F *iguring out how to depict 'indifference' posed a bit of an issue for awhile. I remember quite clearly that at the time I was reading passages from Mara Freeman's* Celtic Spirit *book. So often when I seek inspiration for my paintings, I crack open her book and just begin reading. It's marvelous! In most cases, however, the text is filled with ways to embrace the seasons and make the most of what is at hand. So in thinking it over, I decided to take the opposite approach and have a figure walking away from a pile of carefully placed stones as if she were beginning a new endeavor, a journey. I chose somber greens, browns and golds, and in the end was quite pleased with the results. Interestingly, this image has frequently been sold as a print or greeting card. I think, despite its forlorn mood, many people relate to the necessity of moving on and feeling indifferent to their past efforts. There is always a glimmer of light on the new horizon!*

This card celebrates virtuous indifference to the opinion of others. As Holly noted, the Nine of Stones is about neatly arranging "past efforts," efforts made in the pursuit of happiness, and then walking away toward the rising sun to discover the *happiness of pursuit*. This gesture is as shamanic as it is stoic. It lays claim to virtue through acts of selflessness and surrender—the act of letting go.

This may not be something for everyone to do, but it is something for everyone to think about. Wisdom can be gained by simply contemplating and weighing the merits of such a journey as well as taking one. In readings this card is about neatly ordering life's material and spiritual priorities. It's about renunciation, detachment and refusing to grasp for things. It's about simplifying your life.

The nine stones represent mixed memories of joy and despair; love and fear, gain and loss, regret and acceptance, blame and forgiveness, attachment and detachment, selflessness and self-centeredness, trust and distrust, and surrender and control. The last stone may be the hardest to renounce; we like to be, or like to pretend to be, in complete control of our lives. On a true Hero's Journey, whether existentially or allegorically, such control is impermissible.

The young lady in the Nine of Stones answered the call of her inner shaman. Her load is light; she carries no preconceived notions of how life ahead will unfold. She is indifferent to expectations and content with acceptance. She is simultaneously one with nature and the universe, and the energy of both flow through her.

Cards numbered nine in tarot often mean bringing something to conclusion. The impetus to do so may be rational or emotional depending on the individual. Either way will be fine.

TEN OF STONES

I was sorry when I reached the end of the Stones suit because green has always been my favorite color and I love using it in paintings. But if there must be a final card, then this one was truly a treat! I had fun depicting this sprite and her ten lovely selenite crystals. Green selenite is fairly rare, so she keeps a tight grip on them. I wanted the sprite to be clingy and possessive but also loveable so the viewer could imagine there was hope for redemption. Green selenite is a wonderful stone to keep by one's side while making difficult choices or seeking new friends. It's also helpful when adapting to change. Perhaps there's hope for our little sprite, after all. I found so many inspirational pictures of fairies and sprites that it was great fun hunting through them all. I should also mention that the Celtic theme seemed to play out a lot in the Stone suit. I imagine this was mostly a subconscious response to all the green in the memories of my visits to the Emerald Isle.

Selenite comes in many colors and was named after the Greek moon goddess, Selene. The moon plays an important role in our little sprite's ability to detach herself from her possessions and deny them further power over her.

Tarot cards numbered ten mark the end of a cycle that builds a bridge to something new. The something symbolized by the Ten of Stones is a new worldview balanced between the material and spiritual realms.

This empowering new worldview that is now unfolding across the globe decreases the burdens of the materialistic worldview and increases awareness of the living universe worldview where matter and spirit are equally important. In quantum theory, everything in our universe is interconnected and entangled just like our sprite's hair.

The transformation to a living worldview implies engagement with the numinous, the unseen realms. Such engagements take many forms: tarot readings, synchronicity, visions, dreams, and aha moments of enlightenment. The process sometimes begins with a thunderbolt and at other times with a polite tap on the shoulder. Regardless, both are clarion calls to take stock of core beliefs and priorities.

Selenite and the moon play a significant role in personal transformation. Selenite as a vibrating crystal promotes mental clarity and healing. It has long been associated with transformation. The moon symbolizes the relationship between the material and spiritual realms. The Greek goddess Selene is a personification of the moon.

In readings, the Ten of Stones is a polite tap on the shoulder from the fairy realm by a sprite who fancies mental clarity and selenite. It reminds you to maintain a balance between the material and spiritual realms.

the

ACE OF MIRRORS

The inspiration for the Ace of Mirrors hung in my childhood home for as long as I can recall. At the top of this bronze mirror was the head of Bacchus and beneath it were two sconces. I remember the glass was somewhat tarnished and worn and gave it a lovely antique appearance. As a child, I thought it a very alluring and mysterious treasure. I remember thinking that if one stared long enough into the glass, one might catch a glimpse of the past. This particular mirror watched over all my early artistic pursuits since it hung near an oak dining table where I drew and painted. So when considering the Ace for our Mirror suit, I thought immediately of my childhood antique mirror submerged with sea creatures swimming about to and fro. I decided to feature Daphne, the water nymph, rather than Bacchus. It seemed more fitting to have a feminine presence define the Ace of Mirrors, as suit is predominantly concerned with emotion and creation.

Daphne's Ace of Mirrors is one of the more symbolically detailed cards in Chrysalis. Like all tarot aces, this one represents a new beginning, but a beginning that starts with a cautionary tale about emotional vs. rational choices. As Pascal wrote, *"The heart has its reasons which reason knows not."*

We like to think our decisions are rational, but as often as not they were emotional decisions we later rationalized. Indeed, the heart has reasons that the mind cannot understand. And the heart is more often right than not! So a theme of this ace is to follow your heart.

The sea turtle on the Ace of Mirrors unites Earth and Water elements to buffer emotional tides; the sea plants on either side of the mirror hint at subterranean energy rising from the Collective Unconscious. The spirals on Daphne's headdress symbolize this Otherworldly energy influencing her unconscious mind. The energy is likely hatching a plan that her conscious mind knows virtually nothing about, or at least not yet. The unconscious mind usually marches well in front of conscious decision-making.

When making decisions, the sea snails encourage you to temper your enthusiasm and balance the tides of yin/yang energy. In other words, balance the heart with mind, the emotions with intellect, and the right brain with left brain. One easy way to make your brain function holistically is to cross your arms and legs.

In readings, the two candles next to the snail shells symbolize perfect yin/yang balance. At times they might also symbolize romantic love or a creative endeavor with a non-romantic partner. To better understand what your heart is expressing, allow Holly's treasured bronze mirror to call cherished childhood memories to mind. Doing so soothes the heart, reduces stress and improves mental clarity.

TWO OF MIRRORS

The swans swimming in unison seemed a lovely idea for our Two of Mirrors. It's no secret that when two swans put their heads together, a heart shape is formed. I thought this naturally occurring heart an amazing thing when coupled with the fact that certain bird species mate for life, including geese, swans, cranes and eagles. Apparently, about ninety-percent of bird species are monogamous, which means a male and a female form a 'pair bond.' This makes swans a wonderful symbol for union. I remember taking a stroll the very afternoon I returned from the doctor's office when I was informed I was pregnant. As I passed a nearby pond I asked for a sign that all would be well with my new baby. Well, no sooner had I uttered the words that a swan took flight from beneath the nearby rushes. It remains to this day such a beautiful memory.

Should you draw the Two of Mirrors in a reading be sure to take *swan energy* into consideration. As a spirit animal, a swan awakens the power of self and heightens intuition and awareness, especially in changing times. The Two of Mirrors symbolizes the most reliable centering energy available to us, the energy of unconditional love. It impacts the heart chakra immediately and profoundly, just as the unexpected swan did the day Holly discovered she was pregnant with her daughter, Esme. By the way, Esme's spirit animal is the swan.

The Two of Mirrors symbolizes the bond of sacred balance with lifelong romantic partnerships, as well as union of yin/yang opposites. The two mirrors around the swan's necks reflect the masculine and feminine aspects of the Self onto its partner. It was reflections like these that attracted romantic love in the first place.

In a reading, the Two of Mirrors reminds you that the characteristics of a perfect partnership are not always likely to be present in a relationship. In difficult times compromises often are made to preserve relationship equilibrium. The Two of Mirrors calls to mind all the reasons why the heart is surrendered unconditionally to the safekeeping of another.

The Two of Mirrors asks us to keep our internal yin/yang energies in harmonious balance. This enhances your energy signature. For women, this might mean learning to act more assertively with increased focus. For men, this might mean learning to be introspective and develop intuition by calling on swan's feminine energy.

The Two of Mirrors reminds us the true ability to love others unconditionally requires loving ourselves unconditionally. It requires working through guilt, regret and fear and consciously *choosing* love. According to the sages, love is an act of will not an emotion.

THREE OF MIRRORS

When thinking about the keyword 'compassion,' for the Three of Mirrors, I immediately thought of a lion and a lamb. I'd seen these two beautiful creatures paired together visually when people wished to express compassion and acceptance. And given the fact we preferred not to 'people' our pips, these two seemed likely candidates. I thought it would be exciting to tie an African thread in since Papa Legba is our principal intermediary with the spiritual world. It naturally followed that I would frame the three mirrors with African accents. I remember taking a trip to the Metropolitan Museum of Art in Manhattan around this time. The earth tones and textures of the African art I viewed there are still emblazoned in my mind. What came across mostly was the sense of direct contact with Mother Earth. I have always been so pleased with Chrysalis' earth-centered, multi-cultural vibe!

The African figurine on the Three of Mirrors is named Eshu, a trickster god in the religion of the West African Yoruba People. He is often syncretized with Papa Legba, although in Chrysalis Papa Legba is a spirit guide and psychopomp rather than a trickster. Holly's choice of Eshu as an "African accent" for the Three of Mirrors is an example of the trickster-like synchronicity that characterized the creation of Chrysalis. Readings with Chrysalis cards attract a great deal of synchronicity into your life. That's one of our hallmarks.

The Three of Mirrors in readings symbolizes and celebrates assimilated peoples the world over. It recognizes their rich traditions, love and high esteem for the Earth's sacred mountains, mystical rivers and magical forests. It salutes their ability to adapt and co-exist while maintaining the heart and soul of their parent culture.

This card symbolizes self-acceptance and an urgent need for all populations, assimilated or otherwise, to view themselves through the mirrors of love, compassion and goodwill symbolized by the lion and the lamb. In readings, the Three of Mirrors asks us to examine any *illusions of separation* we harbor and strive to overcome such prejudices. We are all one and we are all connected.

The Three of Mirrors is a card of hope, happiness and optimism. It is a good omen for all things new—romance, business or spiritual adventure. It ignites the twin flames of compassion and altruism that burn with selfless concern for the well-being of others. And it creates awareness of the mystical influences that starve cankers of self-indulgence and nourish virtues of selflessness. These virtues include tolerance, forgiveness, kindness, mercy and humility.

FOUR OF MIRRORS

S ome years ago I completed a painting called Sirene that became very popular. I have often been asked if I would please paint another mermaid. When the keyword 'detachment' came along for the Four of Mirrors, I began to envision an ethereal nymph who was a delicate beauty, yet at the same time distracted and self-absorbed. Remembering that the suit was Mirrors and water was the association, I transformed this nymph into a mermaid, much to the delight of my print customers. I spent some time studying the famous Little Mermaid statue in Copenhagen. I thought it would be a wonderful idea to show four beautiful mirrors propped up around Daphne. But she's too distracted to even bother looking at herself! And, of course, she ignores all the sea life swimming about her. Since it's my habit normally to paint in earth tones, it was a bit of a stretch to complete this piece in shades of blue. I yearned to spice it up with browns and golds.

When one of the Chrysalis *therianthropes* (half-human, half-animal creatures) turns up, it asks that you determine which half best applies to you in this particular reading. All have special gifts. Daphne's mermaid aspect, for example, indicates prophecy. She was named after Daphnis, one of three nymph sisters known in Greece as the *Trinity of Maidens*. They gave the gift of prophecy to Apollo.

The aquatic half of Daphne is emotionally independent and indifferent to material trappings. The human half of her, or him in the case of a merman, is predisposed to episodes of emotional isolation, or drowning self-absorption. The comb and mirrors symbolize Daphne's vanity and she uses them often.

But therianthropes are shapeshifters and consequently symbols of shamanic healing and transformation. All are positive cards. They say, "Cultivate your gifts," whether it's prophecy, clairvoyance, or another sixth sense, and become skilled at dancing between worlds. The emotional, fishy side of Daphne lends itself well to psychic talents.

Seers, visionaries and tarot readers find their human egos at times can pose a challenge. They must take pains to control the noise and itchings of the ego that feed pompous self-absorption. That means avoiding the appearance of being introverted, aloof and wise beyond words. When the sea turtle nudges Daphne, he reminds her to starve her earthbound ego and nourish her natural compassion and congeniality.

Daphne's shadow-side is fickle and as slippery as a fish. Her shadow is a saboteur par excellence, so Daphne-types need to safeguard their relationships by always flying true colors with saintly patience. If Daphne appears often, take care you are not unwittingly sabotaging a relationship you want to hold on to.

FIVE OF MIRRORS

*O*ne of the greatest challenges for me while painting Chrysalis was how to incorporate mirrors, scrolls, spirals or stones into my various paintings. In the case of the Five of Mirrors and the keyword 'forgiveness,' Quan Yin immediately came to mind. As an Asian deity of mercy, I believed she'd make a marvelous fit. Loosely translated, one form of her name means, 'Observing the cries of the world.' Before painting her, I glanced through many renditions until I came upon a few that visually defined what I wished to portray. The next challenge was to conceive a way to include the five mirrors. After a good deal of brainstorming, it dawned on me that since Quan Yin was usually shown seated in the center of a lotus blossom, the large lotus petals might make marvelous mirrors. I must admit, I felt this was very clever of me!

Quan Yin's five lotus flower mirrors represent love, compassion, mercy, forgiveness and self-discipline. All are qualities of the Great Mother and all symbolize noble pathways to enlightenment and self-transformation.

Quan Yin in particular symbolizes the Divine Feminine attributes of forgiveness, mercy and compassion, the qualities discovered through the mirrored light of personal introspection. Late each afternoon the lotus flower closes to reopen again each morning, thereby mimicking the regenerative cycle of birth, death and rebirth. The pink lotus, the lotus that Quan Yin cradles over her heart chakra, symbolizes the beating heart of enlightenment and the purity of divine mercy.

Many Chrysalis cards symbolize the attributes of the Divine Feminine. In addition to Quan Yin, these include Gaia, the Moon, Ariadne, Storyteller, Kali and Sekhmet and the Muse Troupe archetype. Quan Yin is, however, the only one with a mantra—*"Om Mani Padme Hum."* When chanted aloud or repeated silently to oneself in thought or prayer, this invocation pays homage to Quan Yin. It implores her help and counsel and petitions divine assistance from all other Mother Goddesses as well.

Om Mani Padme Hum transforms the impurities of body and mind, just as the lotus flower, which grows in mud, transforms mud into a beautiful flower. In readings, the Five of Mirrors reminds you to delight in the mercy of your own divinity. The quest for purity of heart is accomplished by granting divine mercy to those who have wronged you. The Authentic Self can then rise from the mud of self-righteousness.

The earliest statues of Quan Yin depicted her as a semi-masculine or androgynous figure. Today she embodies the noblest qualities of both. Remember, yin/yang energies are present in each of us. Quan Yin is protectress of all people and hears those who cry out to her.

SIX OF MIRRORS

If memory serves, the Six of Mirrors was the first pip card I painted. I was very excited when it dawned on me I could use natural occurrences of water in nature to serve as reflective mirrors. So, with this in mind I decided upon a scene featuring a spirited sidhe playing Pan Pipes in front of six memory reflecting pools. I have always been fascinated by Pan and such spirits, a fascination that began in childhood when my mother read "The Wind in the Willows" to me. Although not a key character in Kenneth Grahame's beloved book, Pan was still very memorable. He wasn't just a nature god; he was a respectable presence, friend and helper. I felt such a presence was evocative of nostalgic musing and pipe music, two key ingredients for reminiscing.

A sidhe (pronounced shee) is an esteemed fairy whose ancestors belong to the Tuatha de Danaan, the children of the goddess Danu and the old gods of Ireland. Sidhe often are referred to as the *Shining Ones*. Actually, on the Six of Mirrors we see two sidhe; one plays the pipes while the other circles high above the Chrysalis Shrine to the Ancestors. The Shining Ones, as you see, are esteemed shapeshifters.

The rainbow parrot and sidhe piper make merry by serenading visitors who make pilgrimages to the shrine to honor their ancestors. When this card appears in a reading, that visitor might represent you! The six reflecting pools symbolize the healing power of memories awakened by the pipes. They represent dance, color, meditation, relaxation, natural beauty and emotional awareness, also called emotional intelligence.

Collectively, we named the reflecting pools the Pools of Vision. Shamans often describe visions of the sidhe as encounters with wispy, luminescent beings. In Chrysalis the sidhe, as well as all Gentle Fae Folk, serve as intermediaries with our ancestors. They let us know that the best way to honor the ancestors is to achieve our full potential and purpose in life and recover our destiny. The sidhe and ancestors have no greater wish for us.

Chrysalis opens the portal to ancestral communication and mediation through synchronicity, dreams and memories. The benevolent and empowering spirits of the ancestors are always eager to help us discover our personal pathway to enlightenment. Everyone has loving ancestors who wish to see their future generations flourish.

The water in the Pools of Vision flows from an ancient holy well beneath the shrine. The Gentle Folk built a community altar to the ancestors inside the shrine they hope will encourage us to nourish meaningful ancestral relationships in our homes. In return, the ancestors bestow motivation to persevere in the quest to attain our highest goals.

SEVEN OF MIRRORS

*T*he keyword for this card is discernment. My painting focuses on the specific moment when the Lady of Shalott glances away from her loom and sees Sir Lancelot through the forbidden window in her towered prison. She knows that reflected images are but shadows of the real world. This metaphor makes it clear that mirrored reflections are poor substitutes for experiencing life directly. 'I am half-sick of shadows!' she says. The mirror cracks. 'The curse is come upon me,' she cries. An interesting little anecdote is that while I painted this card, I lit candles and listened to Loreena McKennitt's musical rendition of Lord Alfred Tennyson's poem for atmosphere and inspiration.

In Chrysalis readings, the Lady of Shalott serves as a metaphor for many things. Like famous poems and great paintings, tarot cards inspire varied insights and interpretations. The Lady of Shalott lives life imprisoned in a tower overlooking King Arthur's Camelot. She spends her days weaving a tapestry, listening to Camelot's faint music in the distance, and watching others enjoy their boundless freedom. A wicked curse was laid upon her—should she dare leave her tower, she will surely perish.

The Seven of Mirrors calls to mind two things we can never seem to escape: difficult dilemmas and cloudy choices that warp judgment and discernment by blurring reality. As Holly noted, "Mirrored reflections are poor substitutes for experiencing life directly." Certainly, the shadows cast by seven mirrors are far too many blurs to endure. This card helps you discern that one Goldilocks mirror that reflects life clearly and illuminates choices "just right for you."

Perhaps our lady was imprisoned and cursed by the mirrors of history. Her bleak destiny is to weave a tapestry memorializing the glorious victories claimed by male heroes, but never of her own victory. Fortunately, curses find no quarter in tarot readings. The discernment symbolized by this card simply points to taking a risk, sometimes a huge risk. The choice boils down to live life on your own terms or on someone else's.

The empty vessel beneath the loom symbolizes the *passive* pursuit of destiny. The Seven of Mirrors asks this question, "Shall I take this risk or not?" When the mirror cracks, the Lady bids farewell to her tower and the island of Shalott and rows down the river to Camelot. But first she triumphantly wrote her name upon the boat. That gesture was her declaration of freedom that symbolized the *active* pursuit of destiny. In life, destiny will always be paired with freedom.

The Seven of Mirrors is a reminder to seize the freedom of choice that is your birthright and weave the tapestry of your own destiny.

EIGHT OF MIRRORS

This was one of the most magical and transforming cards for me personally. I was in a quandary for some time as to how I might depict 'selflessness.' One evening a vision of a seer or prophet came to me. I saw him walking in desolate mountains. Behind him a meandering path symbolic of his experiences appeared. I was reminded of the ancient Celts whose mummified remains had been found in various places in Asia. In fact, my visualization was probably based on my reading about the Tocharian mummies discovered in China. In any case, our Celtic vate's decorative walking stick was meant to be his only earthly possession. I wanted the painting to impart a feeling of contentment and impartiality. The mirrors make a fascinating statement because they are multi-purposeful; they reflect both the wisdom and experiences we encounter.

The spiritual influences we wrote and painted into Chrysalis Tarot pay tribute to four great tributaries of wisdom that animate the deck. These four tributaries—Eastern (Hindu and Buddhist), Western (Celtic and Greek), African (Egyptian and Vodun) and Indigenous (First Nation and Aboriginal)—shape the style and substance of Chrysalis.

The shaman featured on the Eight of Mirrors, as Holly notes, is a Celtic vate (shaman) who follows Arianrhod of the Silver Wheel. Arianrhod's image graces the top of his walking stick and symbolizes the message of the eight mirrors. She herself is an ancient moon goddess and daughter of Danu, the titular and spiritual Mother Goddess of Celtic people for whom the River Danube was named.

The word Celtic means different things to different people. Celts are most frequently associated with Ireland, but Ireland lays claim to only a small slice of their rich history. Cornwall, Brittany, Scotland and Wales were also once proud Celtic nations. The city of Paris was named for the Celtic Parisii tribe, and Belgium for a confederation of Celtic tribes called Belgae. We find Celtic place names all over Europe and Asia Minor.

Celtic populations in the British Isles can be traced to 3000-4000 BCE, much earlier than once thought. Celtic culture flourished in Europe and expanded southward down the Atlantic Seaway from Scotland to the Mediterranean. The Tocharian mummies discovered in China that Holly mentions had red hair and blue eyes! They came from clans of the extended Celtic family collectively known as Indo-Europeans.

In readings, the Eight of Mirrors are signposts for the wisdom of ancient Celtic spirituality meshed into the meandering path. Celtic spirituality was woven throughout the fabric of Chrysalis Tarot. The card's eight mirrors reflect Arianrhod's silvery light upon the eight noble pathways to enlightenment: selflessness, truthfulness, harmlessness, mindfulness, respectfulness, goodness, peacefulness and righteousness.

NINE OF MIRRORS

This was an easy and delightful card to illustrate! I thought immediately of a book my mother gave me called "Flower Fairies" by Cicely Mary Barker. Cicely's fairies are simply enchanting and were the inspiration for our flower genies. I recalled a recurring conversation with my mother about how, whenever she felt gloomy or depressed, she would seek out a spot in the woods to peacefully observe the trees. Oftentimes there was tension at home and this was my mother's escape. She would tell me that just watching gentle breezes toss the leaves and branches, or observing the sunlight glinting off the dark limbs, spelled pure joy for her. When illustrating the Nine of Mirrors, I thought of those wonderful old trees and felt I should honor my dear mum. The next bit was easy. A light spring shower provided the nine raindrops needed for my mirrors. I then added two flower genies full of joy dancing about in the Tree of Life.

The Nine of Mirrors is Chrysalis Tarot's wish fulfillment and personal empowerment card. Genies are the traditional wish-granters we read about in fables and fairy tales. Our two genies are making their second Chrysalis appearance on this card. Well, sort of. They were still locked tightly away in their bottles in the Golden Flower mandala artwork, a card to inspire meditation.

The moral of the Nine of Mirrors is to become spiritually grounded via meditation or some other mindfulness-based technique such as yoga, reiki or breathwork before letting the genies out of their bottles. When well grounded and centered, we can filter out superfluous and potentially confusing energy patterns and become better able to make informed wishes. It's always better to embrace what destiny wishes for us than to hunger and thirst after worldly desires. The clarity of inner guidance is greatly increased by spiritual grounding.

The Nine of Mirrors is designed to awaken sleeping memories of carefree youthful days spent frolicking in the rain. Recalling cherished memories peels away stress hormones from the body that cause anxiety and illness. Learning to manage stress through spiritual growth and grounding is a Chrysalis wish for everyone.

In readings, the Nine of Mirrors invites you to reconnect with nature just as Holly's mom used to do. Allow the genies and Gentle Folk to guide your way. Our two genies are tree and forest fairies known as dryads. In Chrysalis, fairies are nature spirits. Other nature spirits prefer streams and wells and still others are partial to mountains and valleys. All these Gentle Folk are Green Man's precious children who nurture cherished memories and make wishes come true.

TEN OF MIRRORS

Painting the Ten of Mirrors brought to mind a dove carrying the traditional olive branch. Of course in this case we needed ten doves, so instead of the customary olive branch, I decided on a ribbon all ten birds could share. Releasing doves often commemorates important milestones in life. They symbolize peace and hope at birthdays, weddings and funerals. I wanted the painting to be classically beautiful, and spreading joy is a wonderful visual. In my research I came across a reference to the sport of flying homing pigeons. Pigeons were used in Ancient Greece to proclaim the winner of the Olympics. Mediterranean countries operated an intricate system of watchtowers that included pigeon posts. I'm not certain those ancient messages were as positive as those in Chrysalis. However, what better way to spread peace and hope than with pigeons and doves?

In readings, the Ten of Mirrors bears not only a message of peace and hope but it encourages acceptance and surrender. The universe, after all, is unfolding just as it should. There is no need to exert undue control, especially if this card is present. The Ten of Mirrors represents joy, surrender and acceptance.

Since tens herald an end of a cycle, this ten acknowledges that great progress has been made in controlling emotions and finding peace within. The Ten of Mirrors is a reminder to renounce negative emotions that get in the way of good health and joy. It's also a reminder that we humans share a responsibly to embrace change, grow in knowledge, and make necessary revisions to cherished worldviews, lest we stagnate.

In a changing world, worldviews must be reshaped to reflect new realities and advanced understanding. Outmoded identities need to be relinquished, although that's hard to do. The Aquarian worldview is symbolized by the ribbon that binds together the energies of emotion, sentiment and reality. These energies, if we don't repel them, will help us surrender to change.

Change is always stressful. On the magnitude of an age-ending paradigm shift, the changes we will face pose challenges no one alive today has ever faced. In fact, change of this magnitude last happened well over 2,000 years ago. Chrysalis Tarot was created for the future Age of Aquarius, not the present Age of Pisces. It was designed to help endure and make sense of the turmoil of transition.

The Ten of Mirrors is one of the most positive and joyful cards in Chrysalis. The ribbon symbolizes a barrier to waves of doubt and distrust that seek to dislodge inner peace. The message of the ribbon is that the emotional cycle represented by the Ten of Mirrors is unfurling just as it should.

ACE OF SPIRALS

*A*ries *the ram was one of many real life spirals I chose to represent this suit. It's amazing how many examples of spirals can be found in nature: flower petals, seed heads, pinecones, tree branches and shells serve as good examples. Some keywords for the ram as a spirit animal are force, drive and courage. These traits seemed desirable and compatible with Chrysalis' keyword 'energy.' Interestingly some weeks before I sketched the ram in his feather headdress, my daughter Esme was at work on a project to design a mythical beast. Watching her progress, I became inspired to combine two animals in one and create my own magical beast. The feathered headdress held native and tribal connotations for me. I felt it would lend a certain ram-like power to our representation.*

Many Chrysalis cards are wrapped with an oracular layer powered by a spirit animal, including three of our aces. The Ace of Spirals' spirit animal is Holly's mythical beast. He displays the dual aspects of the ram's cosmic energy and the shaman's tribal magic.

As a card that symbolizes a new beginning, the Ace of Spirals represents the energy of personal growth and the alchemical magic of spiritual transformation. The intention of this ace in readings is to direct attention to goal setting as influenced by the Collective Unconscious. The Otherworld *informs* your intentions by speaking to you through your inner voice. It helps you set goals.

All the other cards in the Suit of Spirals combine the energy of the ram and the magic of the shaman. The Spirals assist you with goal setting while assuring you that your intentions are purposeful because they were inspired by cosmic wisdom. The Otherworld plants desire and then grants accomplishment consistent with personal destiny. Should we wander off the path, the Otherworld steers us back.

When any ace appears in a reading, it represents seeds of a new cycle. For the seeds to sprout and grow to their full potential they must be nurtured physically by the Stones and emotionally by the Mirrors; they must be pruned by the intellect of the Scrolls and nourished by the vibrating energy of the Spirals. Each budding cycle of growth brings you one step closer to the flower of Higher Self.

The Ace of Spirals is a card of manifestation, as are all the Spiral cards. With manifestation, intentions powered by desire are everything. Spirals resonate with divine energy, the sublime energy of the Otherworld. They inform your intentions to help you discover your purpose and passion in life. In readings, the Ace of Spirals heralds new ideas, fresh inspirations and stimulating opportunities.

TWO OF SPIRALS

Here a little wren is trying to decide which nest would serve her better. The male house wren is always the first to arrive in the spring to survey the land and lay claim to the nesting area. When his female partner arrives, she inspects the structure, just as she is doing in my painting. Next she will line the nest with tender grass, bits of bark and soft feathers. Interestingly, the female often hides a sac of spider eggs to help ward off the growth of parasites in her nest. I suppose I favor wrens because I remember my mother being so delighted when they returned each spring to nest near our country cottage. One pair built their home in the eaves of the cottage while another sought out the wooden birdhouse built by my father and attached to an old mulberry tree.

The nests in the Two of Spirals, the Chrysalis suit empowered with life-force creative energy, represent two resources in our quest to know the unknowable and gain divine insight. These two resources are *symbol* and *metaphor*. They inspire active, creative imagination whether used to create a tarot deck or interpret a tarot reading.

Some philosophers believe imagination rather than reason is our highest faculty. Einstein wrote, "Imagination is more important than knowledge." We agree. Chrysalis Tarot is the result of active imaginations informed not by reason or intellect but by symbols and metaphors from in the Collective Unconscious.

The spirals imprinted on the nests are two-dimensional representations of three-dimensional vortices. They symbolize the feedback-feedforward communication we can have with the Collective Unconscious (discussed in Chapter 3). The vorticular spiral on the left spins counterclockwise and *expands outward* into the dark oceans of the Otherworld. The spiral on the right spins clockwise and *collapses inward* into the divine center of Self.

This feedback-feedforward loop accommodates spirited two-way conversations with the Otherworld. Tarot expands the mind into the unseen realm so we can ask questions and intuit the answers. The exchange of information with the Otherworld is one of many factors taken into consideration when we make freewill decisions.

We locate the center of Self with the heart chakra. The choices that lie before us, although informed by the Otherworld, are frequently determined by the heart. As humanist Robert Valett wrote, *"The human heart feels things the eyes cannot see and knows what the mind cannot understand."*

When making important choices, the Two of Spirals asks you to do what the wren is doing. She is weighing her options. After you weigh yours, you can turn tough choices over to the brain's active imagination and the heart's sympathetic intuition.

THREE OF SPIRALS

When I was younger I saw many statues of monks staring out from the gnarled roots of strangler fig trees in Cambodia's Khmer temple and always thought them fascinating. One could almost feel the sweltering heat of the jungle after a sprinkling of rain, and yet the expressions on the faces were unchanging. I remember a friend invited me to visit her family's sculpture garden. I recall the carved stone faces were almost completely overrun with ivy and grasses. In any case, the serene expression on our monk's face made him a perfect subject for our contemplation card. To those familiar with romantic images of ancient religious ruins, the gargantuan tree roots are considered a significant threat. They can split walls, topple building stones and crush intricate carvings. It's a wonder our monk appears unaffected, but then contemplation is a pathway to serenity and acceptance!

We decided our "Buddha in a Bodhi Tree" would depict a contemplative monk from the Cambodian temple of Angkor Wat, the largest religious monument in the world. By featuring Angkor Wat we wished to call attention to geometric alignments found throughout the ancient world. Stonehenge, the Sphinx and Angkor Wat all have linear alignments with the rising sun on the spring equinox.

Angkor Wat is also located on another alignment that spans the circumference of the globe. Within less than one degree of latitude are located the Great Pyramid, Sphinx, Machu Picchu, Easter Island, the lost city of Petra, the Ancient Sumerian city of Ur and Angkor Wat. Many researchers conclude these alignments are evidence of an ancient and lost civilization highly skilled in astronomy, engineering and construction; a civilization keenly aware of the existence of subtle earth energy and nature-based spirituality.

The Bodhi tree in the Three of Spirals is a heuristic symbol, a symbol that prepares you to learn something important about yourself. *Bodhi*, a Sanskrit word, means enlightenment. The Buddha, it's said, attained enlightenment while contemplating under a Bodhi tree, a symbol of prosperity and long life.

But the Buddha is not the only spirit that makes Angkor Wat sacred. The *neak ta*, nature spirits related to the ancestors, and other spirits of the forest known as *bang bat* can be found at grand temples. Temples with the most grandeur claim the most neak ta spirits. Neak ta are healers and mediums that divine the cause of troubles.

In readings, the neak ta and Three of Spirals encourage frequent meditation, an appreciation of sacred space and a deep reverence for the Earth. Contemplation is the key to unlocking an inquisitive mind to the beauty of spiritual understanding and enlightenment.

FOUR OF SPIRALS

This little cottage in the deep dark woods is probably my favorite painting in the Chrysalis deck. There are many beautiful cards, but this one always seems so satisfying. The four fiddlehead ferns seemed a perfect fit for our spiral display. I must confess, when I was researching this piece I felt as if I were house hunting for a future life in a fairy tale. Painting the cottage provided a chance to pull from the myriad of beautiful children's book images I amassed over the years. Interestingly, I found a picture of a round artist's studio in Vermont very inspiring. I came across it one morning and by chance ran into the builder himself. He said it was 'a hand-sculpted work of art, crafted in an eco-friendly, eco-conscious manner.' Our conversation that morning spurred me onward!

We call this the *Harvest Home*, and it has become iconic with Chrysalis. At Holly's suggestion, the Harvest Home is the cover art on the Little White Booklet that accompanies every Chrysalis deck. But this tableau is iconic for other reasons as well, reasons that encompass making room for the new energies and fresh ideas. There's a broom near the front stoop that's perfect for sweeping out the old ideas.

When paradigms shift and worldviews change, the adjustments bring about the difficult process of clearing. *Clearing energy* is one of the subtle energies the Four of Spirals symbolizes in a reading. It is the same renewing energy encountered at an organized spiritual retreat that encourages self-emptying. We call this multi-layered clearing energy *regathering*. Small, like-minded groups and tribes from all over the planet are regathering to celebrate the passion for truth and change.

Another layer of regathering energy is the energy of *communitas,* a Latin word that describes an unstructured community built upon shared liminal or mystical experiences. The subtle energies of ancestors and fairies represent yet another regathering layer. We believe ancestors and fairies find the Harvest Home's serenity and openness to be very welcoming.

The most delicate and unassuming energy found in the universe, that of the Divine Feminine, is symbolized by the Four of Spirals' crescent moon. The moon bathes the Harvest Home with the light of the Divine Feminine who makes all things new. The first crescent in a new moon blooms with the fresh scent of a new tomorrow.

The challenges posed by most anything new are lessened by the clearing energies of regathering symbolized by the Four of Spirals. In readings, the Harvest Home asks you to sweep out antiquated ideas and beliefs that no longer serve you well to make room for those that will.

FIVE OF SPIRALS

My first thought for the keyword 'shadow' was some manner of flame or bonfire. That little flicker of inspiration slowly evolved into five fiery spirals. Oftentimes, I will carry an idea around with me for a day or so and mull it over until I create a satisfying vision. Combining spirals with shadows proved an interesting challenge. I knew I wanted to include a dragon in Chrysalis' lineup and this card provided a perfect opportunity. The deep cavernous walls of the dragon's stony lair provided a wonderful backdrop for the five shadows. In many cultures, dragons are symbols of power and might; however, there is one fundamental difference between European and Asian dragons. European dragons are menacing, and renowned for their destructive ways, whereas Asian dragons are typically benevolent creatures.

The Hero's Journey is among the most harrowing of personal psychological pursuits. That's because spiritual growth must be hardened over the flames of psychic healing—and here be dragons! Journeys of self-discovery hold joys and delights yet are fraught with challenges and crossroads deliberately put on your path to dragoon spiritual growth. The Five of Spirals is about shadow work, and shadow work is work we don't enjoy thinking about.

But it's necessary. The shadow-self, the aspect of the psyche that's hidden and even denied, is the home of disavowed negative energy patterns. We know the negativity is there but we deny it by projecting its characteristics onto other people, just as our dragon is projecting the shadows of negative energy patterns onto his canyon wall.

To assist you with shadow work, Holly painted a meditation mandala on the dragon's wing. One key to shadow work is to name and claim your shadow issues and meditation will help uncover their hiding place. Shadow work is important because it transmutes negative weaknesses into positive strengths.

Many shadow issues can be traced to primitive instincts and religious stigmas. These include guilt, lust, selfishness, greed, anger, resentment, and envy. We call them "our demons." When we consider something's evil and unacceptable, and then deny it, we send it to the dark side. Everyone has a dark side.

The word *dragon* comes from a Greek term that means to see things clearly. As your fierce advocate and guardian spirit, the dragon keeps vigil high above your soul. As you name and claim a demon, the dragon's fiery breath engulfs whatever your psyche purges.

Psychologist Stephen Diamond writes in *Meeting the Shadow, "When we give voice to our inner demons...we transmute them into helpful allies in the form of newly liberated, life-giving psychic energy."* This liberated psychic energy makes us more considerate and compassionate toward others. Shadows dissolve whenever light is cast upon them.

SIX OF SPIRALS

*A*pink clootie was my inspiration for the Six of Spirals. One often finds ritual clooties hanging on the branches of trees near holy wells. Painting this card held special meaning for me because I participated in the ritual long ago. I was living in Asia at the time and visited many temples where the faithful left offerings to enhance chances that their prayers were heard. I did this very thing when I lived in Hong Kong and was eager to adopt a baby girl. Upon learning of the various difficulties of adoption in Hong Kong, I wrote my wishes down on a pink piece of fabric and hung it from the only tree in my yard. Within two weeks, I received news a source in the Philippines had found a baby girl for me. That beloved child, Gabrielle, is now an adult. As an infant, her arrival in my life and my arms was a dream come true thanks to a pink clootie!*

The keyword for the Six of Spirals is 'success'. This is one of Chrysalis' wish fulfillment cards. Hanging clooties is a powerful means of petitioning the "local spirit" of a sacred place, which would certainly include one's home. A clootie may embody an intention, serve as a votive offering for physical, psychological or spiritual healing, or simply represent a token of thanksgiving for wishes previously granted.

A ritualized approach to clooties harmonizes intentions with emotions, which is important to manifestation. In Celtic lands, clooties, hawthorn trees and holy wells all evoke the magic of nature. Any sincere ritual accomplishes just as much and serves to power wish fulfillment. Simply imagining the emotional fulfillment your wish will bring you will itself power manifestation.

In readings, the Six of Spirals not only invites you to make a wish, but reminds you to ritualize your wish-making process. This card might also allude to a transition that for now needs to remain hidden in order to ripen. The dual symbolism of the full moon and hawthorn tree, which makes way for new growth by shedding leaves, points to an upcoming transition.

Full moons provide the perfect opportunity to bid farewell to energies that no longer serve you and may now be significant barriers to spiritual progress and manifestation. Meditating on the Six of Spirals illuminates such energy patterns that have outlived their usefulness so you can ceremoniously release them and move on.

The Six of Spirals asks you to draw down the awesome energy of the moon and petition it to shine healing energy and the pink light of unconditional love on those most in need. The moon is a symbol of the Great Mother Goddess who hopes all good things for you.

SEVEN OF SPIRALS

O nce again I had a chance to use a bear, my totem animal, in the pip card lineup. Bears are not particularly ferocious or malicious and have very little desire to interact with humans. They are normally shy and retiring and, unless forced, usually choose to avoid us. But bears, like humans, have a sense of personal space. If threatened or invaded, they defend it. So this background set the stage for the keyword 'assertion.' Another joy this card gave me was a chance to paint spirals as petroglyphs, a subject close to my own heart. At the time I'd just come back from a trip to the Grand Canyon where I also visited the Painted Rock Petroglyphs in southwest Arizona. Spirals, some of the oldest symbols used in spiritual practices, are featured prominently on several rocks there. No wonder our bear defends his decorated lair!

Should you see the Seven of Spirals frequently in readings, the bear may be signaling that he's your spirit animal. Spirit animal attributes are important factors in Chrysalis readings. Bear energy, for example, powers communication between the conscious and unconscious mind and strengthens your intuition and perceptions of the unseen world. Bear energy exhibits great strength and exercises great caution simultaneously.

The Seven of Spirals highlights self-assertiveness, a human quality best administered with bear-like strength and caution. The "Goldilocks" approach to assertiveness balances *strength*, which can lead to overbearing power and control, with *caution*, which can lead to setting weak and fuzzy boundaries. Weak, fuzzy boundaries are the building blocks of codependency. Typically, weak boundaries are unenforced.

The cold porridge of codependency is a significant problem for many people. Its main cause is the lack of self-esteem, which also breeds fear of rejection. Codependents are overly concerned about what others think about them. Establishing balance between caring for yourself and caring for others is the lesson of the Seven of Spirals.

When our bear awakens from his winter's rest, he expects to find *Goldilocks* balance was restored to his surroundings. In our own surroundings it's important to maintain balance between the hot porridge of aggressive, outspoken behavior (strength) and the cold porridge of passive, reserved behavior (caution).

When assertiveness is just right, your energy signature will attract like-minded individuals into your life. You'll finally meet the people you were destined to meet and foster strong relationships with them. Assertiveness means protecting sacred space, setting clear boundaries, and accepting responsibility for the choices you make.

If you persevere and enforce boundaries with the tenacity of the mighty bear, you are bound to prosper. The bear's magical energy inspires incisive introspection, honest self-examination and genuine self-acceptance.

EIGHT OF SPIRALS

*T*his card has always been exceedingly important to me. Just seeing our deer leaping in front of the moon beneath the shooting spirals makes me smile because it reminds me of someone. I'm a great believer in the power of ancestral energy and call upon it when need runs deep. On the heels of three prophetic dreams, I felt a burning need to reconnect with a man with whom I'd enjoyed a romantic but tumultuous relationship. The dreams felt like calls from the Otherworld beseeching me to seek him out. In the three dreams he lay dying. His face was surrounded by an intense white light as he called out to me without words. The dreams warned there was no time to lose. During a quickly arranged visit we enjoyed a healing rendezvous. One month later he died!

The Eight of Spirals is the Chrysalis dream awareness card. It reminds you to be mindful of your waking and sleeping dreams, and of odd inspirations and mysterious impulses. Taking the phase of the moon into consideration when such inspirations occur will often enhance dream interpretation. For example, the Hunter's Moon pictured here occurs in October around the time of the Celtic festival of Samhain, which honors the ancestors.

During Samhain, the forerunner of Halloween, the veil between the worlds is lifted. Ancestral energy from the Otherworld can flow freely and be experienced by everyone. Sudden energy shifts pique the attention of the unconscious mind, although we may be unaware of them. Like the regal stag racing through the forest, the unconscious mind races to sort the threads of subtle energy and weave them into timeless dreamscapes.

Dreams and tarot are kissing cousins; Otherworldly inspirations are the same for both. Tarot readings inspire dreams as well as illuminate dream interpretation. The meaning of a dream is often rendered more intelligible by a tarot reading. Notable Chrysalis cards associated with dreamwork in addition to the Eight of Spirals include shamanic archetypes such as Storyteller, Papa Legba, the Watcher and the Dreamer.

Another dimension of the Eight of Spirals is symbolized by the stag, the Lord of the Forest. He may be your personal spirit animal. Stag connects the past and present with the future, as he did in Holly's three pre-cognitive dreams. He brings to mind challenges and unresolved matters that require timely attention.

When not appearing as a spirit animal, the stag heralds a momentous change or experience that will enrich your life. Cards numbered eight in Chrysalis are mystical, magical cards. They increase awareness of the past, promote responsibility for growth in the present, and inspire dreams and visions of the future.

NINE OF SPIRALS

*O*ne of the lovely things about growing up in an artistic household is you never know what you'll stumble across next—visually speaking. There was a treasure trove of odds and ends in our Manhattan brownstone: old books, card decks, dried flowers and handmade miniature villages. Especially memorable was a collection of old maps my parents had amassed. I was always fascinated by them and often tried to find present day sites. It was here I first discovered the Anemoi, the Greek wind deities. I just loved this idea and especially the depictions. They were sometimes represented as mere gusts of wind, at other times were personified as winged men, and at still other times were depicted as horses kept in the stables of Aeolus. So when faced with the keyword 'perseverance,' I thought immediately of my old friends the wind gods!

When Aeolus sails into a reading, he indicates that the present cycle is in its final stage. All cards numbered nine in tarot foretell completion, so this can be a helpful card when you're attempting to figure out what's going on and what comes next in your life. Look to adjacent cards for symbols pointing to a new beginning, important information or needed reflection.

Aeolus himself is the great cosmic organizer and Keeper of the Winds. Odysseus sought his help during his voyage home to Ithaca and was granted fair winds. The voyage "home to Ithaca" is one of many metaphors for the Hero's Journey, whose goal is to transcend the ego and shine beacons of light upon the Higher Self.

In the beginning, our essence was whole and the term Higher Self had no practical meaning. Higher Self and Psyche were fully integrated. At birth, the psyche was fractured into *Ego Self* and *Higher Self* and the seeker's quest to return to the light of Higher Self began.

Life's Holy Grail demands perseverance in the quest to recover your Higher Self, which is another term for your destiny. This quest is a constant struggle to calm the disruptive winds of ego and attain enlightenment, however the word is defined—cosmic consciousness, spiritual transformation, ascension, etc. All these terms define a process of growing the quality of consciousness.

The Grail itself is symbolized by butterflies, a word that, like soul, means psyche in Greek. Aristotle gave the butterfly the name psyche and called her the "source of thought, perception and belief."

In readings, the Nine of Spirals bodes fair winds and smooth sailing. It advises you to stay the course you set at the beginning of the present cycle, but to be prepared to yield control of your ship to Aeolus for transition to the next cycle.

TEN OF SPIRALS

This half-horse, half-human creature embodies two natures. One might imagine that there is constant conflict for the poor centaur. His human aspect is continuously at odds with untamed animalistic impulses. Aside from the heavy burden our centaur carries, he finds himself at a crossroads faced with a decision. The centaur must decide which path to follow. I must confess I found myself identifying terribly with our over-burdened centaur during the days I painted Chrysalis. His ten spiraled bundles reminded me of all my earthly goods. I was facing an imminent move across country and had an abundance of possessions residing in various storage units. I held much fear at the prospect of letting go of belongings and of being on my own for the first time. However, I found that traveling my own path and facing my fears gave me the release I needed!

Whether a symbol for unneeded possessions or unhealed wounds, the Ten of Spirals is known to anyone once baffled by a burdensome crossroads. However you visualize the centaur's excess baggage, the ten bundles of potentially transformative energy cannot propel you into the next cycle until matters are resolved. Moving forward requires effort, determination and willpower.

Festering emotional wounds are the result of unprocessed pain and anguish. One rolled up bundle might signify the loss of a loved one; another bundle might symbolize regret, anger or resentment. The list is long. These are bundles of fear, raw emotion and negativity that prevent healing because forgiving others can be difficult and forgiving ourselves can be next to impossible.

In a reading, the Ten of Spirals asks that we choose the narrow path, the path of forgiveness. This is the path that overcomes fear and leads to self-acceptance. Choosing this path is the decision to release surplus baggage and the will to see it through. The centaur asks, "Am I a sentient, self-aware human able to make choices and live with them, or am I simply a hard-wired beast of burden and pitiable victim of circumstance?"

The famous Irish playwright George Bernard Shaw wrote, *"People are always blaming their circumstances for what they are. I don't believe in circumstances. The people who get on in this world are the people who get up and look for the circumstances they want, and, if they can't find them, make them."*

You may not know how to "make them," but fortunately your Higher Self does. The Ten of Spirals beckons you to listen to your "inner voice" and trust your instincts and intuition. Doing so will produce a moment of truth when you can declare, "Enough!" In that instant you summon the will to forgive, release baggage and set forth on the high road to healing, enlightenment and self-fulfillment.

ACE OF SCROLLS

I love ravens, so when it came to the Ace of Scrolls I decided a cawing raven would make the perfect emissary for the suit of intuition. As there is a slightly ominous overtone to the suit in general the raven, again, seemed the perfect ambassador. I have read many accounts describing the clever accomplishments of these birds and it seems reasoning and intuition play a key role in many of their endeavors. I added the skeleton keys so the reader would have the ability to unlock doorways that materialized during their ensuing, intuitive journeys. Lastly, when it came to the inscription on the scroll I chose cuneiform as it's one of the earliest known writing systems. The Bronze Age pictographs seemed the perfect way to convey ancient and mysterious messages of discovery and hope on our Ace of Scrolls.

We discovered that when Raven wants to attract your attention, this Ace frequently flies out of the deck. In fact, all animal spirit guides in Chrysalis behave the same way. They do so to announce themselves as one of your spirit animals. Since tarot aces herald new beginnings, maybe one of the Raven's keys is meant to unlock the mystery of shamanic power animals for you. Animal spirit guides provide protection, healing and encouragement when life tosses difficult challenges. Spirit animals enhance our understanding of non-ordinary reality, an important Chrysalis objective.

It was once believed that animal energies aided physical healing, a notion dubbed *animal magnetism*. Medical science, however, uncovered no supporting evidence, so animal magnetism was denounced and, for the most part, forgotten. Yet good things came from Franz Mesmer's 19th century belief system, one being the word *mesmerize*.

Mesmer believed that energy could move freely between animate and inanimate objects. Of course, another century would have to pass by before quantum physics supported his teaching and revealed the truth of an interconnected universe. No shaman today, or even 100 years ago, would ever take issue with Franz Mesmer's insight into the role that animal spirit guides have in healing.

In readings, the Ace of Scrolls underscores one of the more important lessons in Chrysalis: nurturing your intuition so communication with the Otherworld becomes like second nature and part of your ordinary reality. All the Scroll cards are like intuition—airy and subjective. By the way, mesmerism morphed into psychological hypnosis, another key that unlocks the unconscious mind and gateway to the Otherworld.

New ways of thinking always encounter opposition, especially when non-ordinary reality is involved. The Ace of Scrolls says to hold fast to your beliefs and endure ridicule with humility. The world is rapidly changing before our very eyes and many find it unsettling.

TWO OF SCROLLS

The word 'fantasy' conjures up so many different visions. As I mulled over this particular keyword, a few lines from an old Irish folk song by Ralph McTell called "Clare to Here," *kept coming to mind.* "I dream I see white horses dance upon that other ocean. It's a long, long way from Clare to here!" *The notion of seeing white horses dancing on oceans stuck with me. And, as is often the case with an artistic inspiration, this one evolved into something quite different than I first anticipated. The white horses from the Irish folk song became a single black unicorn. I set him to 'dancing' upon two parchment scrolls. I was reminded all along of my daughter Gabrielle who, in her youth, regarded unicorns as the most marvelous of creatures. A unicorn always makes me think of her.*

L ike white horses dancing on an ocean, a unicorn is determined to experience oceans of magic on his own. As a fantastical creature, he's free to dance wherever he likes and to write his own myth and sing his own song. The Two of Scrolls reminds us it's better to experience the unicorn's magical world actively rather than to read about someone else's experience of it passively. Active experience is achieved through active imagination, the creative force that dreams new visions and turns them into reality.

A unicorn senses the unseen world with his horn, the symbol of his third eye. The Third Eye or sixth chakra motifs occur frequently in Chrysalis. That's because musings of the sixth sense give birth to unborn ideas. The unicorn's horn pierces the heavens to actively sense the Otherworld's higher realms.

The Two of Scrolls also emphasizes the importance of maintaining a healthy balance between fantasy and reality when making decisions. Although a unicorn's head is often spotted in the clouds, he keeps two feet on the ground when discerning important choices that affect his life. He's a master of unconventional thinking and counter-intuitive reasoning, so this card in readings likely suggests an unconventional or even impractical approach is worth considering.

The benefits of thinking *into* an obstacle or problem rather than simply thinking *about* it often produce the best result. Thinking holistically into problems illuminates the whole rather than just the parts and develops the big picture. Our lives are shaped by creative and subjective forces that can only be intuited by the Third Eye. The unicorn's horn symbolizes the bridge of perception that connects our world to the Otherworld.

In a reading, the Two of Scrolls asks you to recall a Test of Destiny when everything worked out fine because you boldly chose to zig when conventional wisdom said you must surely zag.

THREE OF SCROLLS

*T*he fox is associated with adaptability and cunning and in many ancient cultures is known to be a shapeshifter. When pondering the keyword, 'rejection', I recalled a beautifully illustrated Yōkai folktale I came across when I lived in Japan. In this ancient tale a handsome young man named Ono spends years searching for a wife. One evening while roaming the countryside he meets a foxy woman named Kitsune. Although she possesses a secret, Ono grows to love and marry her. Unfortunately the family dog becomes more and more hostile to the lady of the manor. She begs her husband to kill the dog but he refuses. One evening the dog attacks Ono's beautiful wife so furiously that she shapeshifts back into a fox and flees. "Please come back to me," Ono called out. So every evening she returns to sleep in his arms. I liked that the sorrow and trauma in this tale was healed by love and romance.

The Three of Scrolls is about healing and soul recovery. Trauma brought about by rejection, betrayal, physical or emotional abuse, acrimonious divorce, the death of a loved one, or other events cause a piece of soul to flee. This is the way the psyche deals with pain; the suffering piece of soul runs away. When it's returned or retrieved, healing begins in earnest. Holly's folktale is an allegory of soul loss and recovery.

Healing from soul loss involves regaining trust, granting forgiveness and overcoming fear. Once the trauma has been released and allowed to pass, the healing process restores lost energy and personal empowerment. It restores willpower and energizes the strength to mend the psyche and return it to wholeness. At one time or another, we all suffer, or have suffered, from soul loss.

In readings, the Three of Scrolls increases awareness of soul loss, which is primarily a spiritual affliction. If left unresolved, soul loss may morph into a physical or mental disease. Indeed, there's a large body of empirical evidence that shows many diseases can be directly linked to soul loss, chronic spiritual disharmony and/or entrenched negative energy.

When a healing card such as the Three of Scrolls turns up in a reading, it may implicate negative energy blocking a chakra. These blockages, as well as negative emotions and stress in general, vibrate at low frequencies that impede cellular function and make us sick. The violet color on the Three of Scrolls symbolizes spiritual healing.

If this card appears often, it may indicate an unhealed wound resulting from soul loss. It could be an incident you swept under the rug and just forgot about because it was so painful. Unhealed psychic wounds have a long-term affect on your joy and well-being and the habit of returning to the surface.

FOUR OF SCROLLS

There are many old tales that revolve around the idea of a character who falls asleep under the influence of a magic spell. The keyword, 'recollection', brought these stories to mind. As far as the painting is concerned, I began to think in terms of a fairy with her memories written upon four parchment scrolls. I was inspired by tales of my great aunt, who was a marvelous writer. She explained that she liked to sleep with a few inspiring bits of prose or poetry inscribed on tiny papers kept beneath her pillow. The idea was these would fuel creative flames for the next day. I decided our fairy could use her recollections however she chose. If troubles were afoot, she might sleep on magic scrolls to help heal her woes.

Recollection heals woes and reduces everyday stress by focusing the mind on moment-to-moment awareness. The word *recollection* simply means thinking nonjudgmentally about how you honestly see yourself through your own eyes. It also means to resist seeing yourself through the judgmental eyes of others. Recollection is defined as meditation on self-acceptance designed to nurture self-esteem and grow personal empowerment.

Our tranquil fairy is curled up with four scrolls that stand for the Four Chrysalis Recollections. They are Mind, Body, Spirit and Feeling. Each scroll is a signpost pointing to a particular recollection pathway. For example, "What is my Body telling me about how it's being cared for?" "What patterns create issues that dominate my Mind?" "What energy source invigorates my Spirit?" "What *unconscious* emotions and feelings do I have that need to be elevated to *conscious* awareness?"

When the Four of Scrolls appears, our tranquil fairy asks you to compose your own personal recollection pathways. This does not necessarily mean recalling past memories. Only Body and Feeling are anchored in the past and present; Mind and Spirit are free to roam the timeless realm. Through recollection, we learn from the timeless realm how to heal past and present afflictions. This information is imparted to us during *meditative consciousness* as infused knowledge.

Meditative consciousness, another term for mindfulness, is about making friends with the present moment and entering into a nonjudgmental relationship with it, rather than just liking it or hating it. Relationshipping with the present moment means embracing the wisdom of the four scrolls. The benefits are many: the mind becomes more stable and less reactive; memory improves; mental clarity and coping mechanisms improve, and you accept that it's perfectly okay to be right where you are now.

The Four of Scrolls is one of Chrysalis' most empowering wellness cards. When this fairy graces your reading, write your recollection pathways on a scroll to place under your pillow.

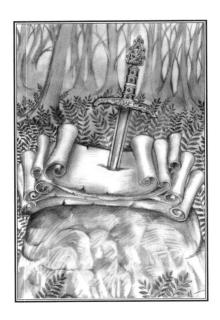

FIVE OF SCROLLS

Despite the dark overtones, I truly enjoyed painting this card. The subject matter and lighting worked well together and the colorful, atmospheric outcome was very pleasing. My inspiration piece was a little Celtic resin plaque featuring a deer that was given to me by an old friend. It resides in a place of honor in my bedroom hall. In order to provide an additional aspect of hope, I painted a background where the lavender light of promise shines vibrantly in the center of the forest. One must always retain hope, even during the most trying of times. Hope is our greatest ally! The card's keyword is 'sacrifice.' Through many trials and tribulations, we can now finally perceive the big picture. Self-sacrifice for loved ones is a small price to pay when the rewards of the future are great.

The forest Holly painted into the background of the Five of Scrolls is named Brocéliande, the legendary forest in France where Merlin is buried. The Sword in the Stone is Excalibur, the magical sword the Lady of the Lake gave to King Arthur. In Chrysalis mythology, the Lady of the Lake is none other than Morgan le Fay, who graces our Sorceress card.

Even today, Brocéliande is still a magical forest and home to the Gentle Fairy Folk of Celtic Brittany. Sir Lancelot was born and reared in Brocéliande Forest. Morgan and her nine sisters raised him to exemplify the five Arthurian virtues of loyalty, courage, hopefulness, compassion and generosity.

In Chrysalis, these five virtues symbolize the sacrifices of the Five of Scrolls. Together, they form the Chrysalis Code of Chivalry. Those who honor the Code are able to extract Excalibur from the stone and return it to the Lady of the Lake. She then will pay it forward to another worthy seeker who follows King Arthur's path.

The Five of Scrolls is Chrysalis Tarot's pay-it-forward card. It asks you to choose hope or one of the other virtues and pay it forward as an act of self-sacrifice. When you pay virtue forward, the universe returns it to you ten-fold. As Holly noted, rewards in your future will be great.

Excalibur is not a vicious instrument of power or vengeance in Chrysalis; it symbolizes self-sacrifice and personal destiny. The steel of Excalibur was tempered to slash through the bramble of proud and pompous egos so the purple light of higher consciousness could illuminate a more appropriate path.

Cards numbered five in tarot point to challenges. The Five of Scrolls recommends that you not fight or resist challenges, but accept them in the light and elegance of the present moment. Although things may seem dark at times, the Five of Scrolls is filled with magic and the promise of hope.

SIX OF SCROLLS

I love elephants! This card's keyword 'consolation' provided me the opportunity to feature one of these enchanting and noble creatures. I rarely choose to press my beliefs on others, but animal's rights, and in particular those of elephants, are dear to my heart. A wonderful woman named Lek Chailert and the elephants in her wildlife park served as my inspiration for this painting. Lek has received great acclaim for her tireless work. She is the founder of the Elephant Nature Park in Chiang Mai where so many animals have found refuge. During the years I painted Chrysalis, I followed Lek's journey, her triumphs and tragedies, through Internet posts. Chrysalis Tarot is all about growth and healing; there is a great need to address these issues when considering man's relationship with animals. Our deck seemed a marvelous vehicle within which to subtly offer this message. The fairy is consoling the elephant and in return he offers her a confirming message of thanksgiving.

Holly's painting on the Six of Scrolls is one of her most popular Chrysalis images. After all, spiritual consolation is something everyone seeks and desires. It's our means of confirming that we're on the right path and making the right decisions—that we're exactly where we're supposed to be.

You can interpret the small scroll the elephant holds in his trunk in many ways. One way is to imagine the fairy is submitting your query for the elephant's counsel and/or confirmation. The words written on the scroll might outline an idea you had, a plan you devised, or the proposed solution to a dilemma. You should actually write down the query on a handy piece of paper to make the magic work.

Spiritual confirmation appears in a variety of ways, and all are consoling. Such confirmation produces peace and tranquility and gives you the willpower to proceed with confidence. Confirming consolation often appears in the form of synchronicity when you least expect it. You will have no doubt when it's a magical response from the Otherworld to motivate you toward destiny.

Synchronicity is magic slipping in and out of time to attract attention at critical moments, just like a signpost. Tarot is a spiritual practice that attracts synchronicity and consolation into your life.

In readings, the Six of Scrolls may point to an obstacle obscuring clear discernment. If that's the case, then this card invites you to devise a plan for getting around it. In Hindu mythology, the beloved elephant Ganesha, the Lord of Success, removes obstacles to personal destiny such as pride, selfishness and vanity. He is closely associated with your first chakra, called the root chakra.

SEVEN OF SCROLLS

This piece was inspired by my childhood memories of C.S. Lewis,' The Lion, The Witch and the Wardrobe. Set in 1940's England, Lucy and her siblings are sent to the countryside to escape the Blitz. Lucy stumbles upon a mysterious wardrobe and climbs inside. Before she realizes what's happening, she disappears behind the coats and emerges into a mystical land called Narnia. Wandering about Narnia's forest she meets Mr. Tumnus, a faun, by a lantern. They go off together for tea at his house. Well, I found the idea of slipping into a mystical land pure delight since my head was always full of beautifully illustrated dreams. Once when I was young, I happened upon a friendly faun who played with me. I remember our gambol to this day, so naturally I loved Lewis' descriptions of the faun's dwelling, belongings, and the snowy forest that enveloped Lucy and Mr. Tumnus.

The following example of synchronicity is a footnote to Holly's story.

In C.S. Lewis' book, Mr. Tumnus scurries about the forest carrying an umbrella and a few rolled up parcels that look very much like scrolls from the Suit of Scrolls. So this Narnian story must be the perfect story to illustrate the dilemma of the faun on the Seven of Scrolls.

The young faun on the card struggles with a tough decision. It's important to mention that fauns are therianthropes—half human and half animal creatures. They can shapeshift to become either fully animal or fully human. As an animal, a faun is hard-wired; his decisions come mostly from instinct. As a human, however, a faun delights in making freewill choices, but like a human can at times be indecisive. 'Indecision' is this card's keyword.

The faun on the Seven of Scrolls invokes counter-intuitive reasoning. Sometimes the most courageous (and correct) decisions go against the grain and appear to make little sense at all. Thankfully, human decision-making involves intuition and emotion as much as logic and intellect.

C.S. Lewis' character of Lucy Pevensie is a sensitive little girl who learned to trust her intuition. She even schooled her older siblings in the art of active or creative imagination. Lucy yearns to dance in the forest with Narnia's nature spirits, the spirits driven away by humans lacking creative imagination. Creative imagination lends a certain air of confidence to counterintuitive reasoning.

This card reminds you that tough choices sometimes require creative solutions inspired by creative imagination. Toward the end of her reign, Lucy the Valiant, then Narnia's queen, allowed creative imagination to lead her back to the lantern where she and Mr. Tumnus first met. Near the lantern she serendipitously discovered a magic portal that returned her safely back to England.

EIGHT OF SCROLLS

*O*ur Egyptian visionary is colorful and clever when reporting psychic forays into the future. We wonder about the eight scrolls though. Are they merely illusions, or do they truly predict the future? Fortune telling, like divination, is the practice of predicting something about someone's life. On my father's side of the family, as with many 'old world' Irish, there was a long history of fortune telling. But my grandmother was the inspiration for this card. She was often graced with prophetic dreams and could 'read the tea leaves.' While my father was serving in WWII, my granny awakened one morning from a fitful dream that he had drowned. It turned out my father, who never learned to swim, had fallen into a river in the Solomon Islands. Luckily he was rescued by one of his buddies!

In the upper realm of the Otherworld, the past, present and future blend together. Your Higher Self, which is your destiny, resides in this realm and is intimately familiar with all three. The Hero's Journey can be regarded as the quest to retrieve the Higher Self. The quest details a cautious adventure into non-ordinary reality to seek "roadside assistance."

The more inflated the ego, the more need there is for roadside assistance. Such assistance is provided by shamans, clairvoyants, psychics, visionaries and other highly perceptive, empathic individuals. The Eight of Scrolls pays tribute to these gifted souls and the sacrifices they make serving others. To paraphrase the words of Mircea Eliade, they responded to the call and found the absolute freedom sought by mortals.

Absolute freedom, according to Eliade, *"is the desire to break the bonds that keep us tied to Earth and to free us from our limitations. Shamans constitute exemplary models for the rest of the community because they have realized transcendence and freedom and have become like spirits."* We each have an "inner shaman" and the response-ability to transcend the Self.

In readings, the visionary reminds you to be practical and conserve an open mind. The daily choices you make for better or worse affect your quest to retrieve destiny. Poor or incorrect choices often detour us to places where a necessary lesson can be learned.

Chrysalis Tarot seeks to heal, empower and inspire. It will never disempower by foisting specific advice about decisions you yourself should make. Chrysalis archetypes are direct lines to destiny and Higher Self; the other cards provide roadside assistance that helps you overcome obstacles. All Chrysalis cards inform your inner voice—your ultimate spiritual director.

The Eight of Scrolls visionary is a wise and friendly sage. Her advice is not to worry, trust the Upper Realm and follow your intuition.

NINE OF SCROLLS

Cemeteries have long been known for their tranquility and architectural beauty. Many a day I spent rambling through the old Gate of Heaven cemetery in Mt. Pleasant, New York when I was a teen. We picnicked there and visited the graves of Babe Ruth, Tommy Dorsey and James Cagney, among numerous others. I was so enamored of the statuary that oftentimes I would go there simply to sketch. Eventually I painted a very large oil painting of a grieving angel. I remember the angels were so beautifully rendered that they might well have been actual models posing for me. Later in life I visited the graveyard in Salem, Massachusetts and its unparalleled array of early American angel and death heads. Though primitive in nature, the early gravestones provided great atmosphere and charm. Needless to say I had much to draw upon when it came to the Nine of Scrolls and 'despair.'

Many of us have experienced mild despair, but it seldom lasted for very long. Paradoxically, seeds of hope sprout from those dark moments as the heart and mind fight the despair and seek to restore balance. The Nine of Scrolls isn't about suffering long-term despair or depression; it's about renewal and the spiritual rewards of self-emptying prompted by suffering.

The Greek word for the self-emptying process depicted on the Nine of Scrolls is *kenosis*. The spiritual practice of kenosis is taught by all religions, usually in abstract doctrinal teachings that refer to a specific act performed by a sage or savior. The Nine of Scrolls teaches self-emptying as an on-going spiritual process. The Otherworld is unable to assist you when your glass is always full.

In Chrysalis, the Hero's Journey frequently speaks of letting go of control in order to harness the ego. Other words for self-emptying heard often in spiritual circles include renunciation and surrender. The objective is to overcome the belligerence of ego by baring the heart to inspiration from the Otherworld. The unseen realm wills nothing for us; it simply wishes to be heard so it can guide us. It always accepts invitations to fill an empty glass.

Self-emptying sometimes requires a mild case of despair to thin the overgrown forest of ego so the seeds of hope can receive light. When the Nine of Scrolls appears in readings, it may be pointing to an overgrown forest—that is to say, an ego that needs to be thinned of self-centered thoughts. Mystics refer to this kind of forestry as the Dark Night of the Soul.

The Nine of Scrolls asks the question, "What does destiny require of me?" By definition, retrieving your Higher Self is your destiny. Destiny always plants new seeds of hope during the darkest nights.

TEN OF SCROLLS

A t the time I tackled the sketch for the Ten of Scrolls, my daughter Esme was painting for a high school art project. Usually Esme comes to me for ideas, but this time I decided I'd turn the tables and follow her lead. Often when I'm painting and can't quite decide what elements to add in the background, or what atmosphere to attempt, I turn my desires over to the universe and wait for the answer. Everything that happens in the universe begins with intention. You imagine your desire as best you can and then release it. I decided upon this small, simple approach when wondering what animal to feature on this card. After the release, I visited my daughter in her room and found her hard at work on a tiger. There was my answer!

E sme's tiger on the Ten of Scrolls symbolizes spiritual acts of letting go and surrender also depicted on other Chrysalis cards,
except in this case the required spiritual energy is confined. Actually
it's bottled and corked in a self-imposed prison because an important
lesson still needs to be learned before the present cycle ends. Otherwise it will just keep on repeating itself until broken once the lesson
is finally learned.

The Ten of Scrolls asks you to identify cycles in your life that
appear to repeat themselves. Are you attracting the wrong people,
for example? Or perhaps the same negative circumstances occur over
and over again? In either case, this has a great deal to do with your
energy signature. You will attract, and keep on attracting, people and
circumstances that mirror the vibrational energy pattern you emit,
which is defined as your energy signature.

Various things have a lasting adverse effect on an energy signature. These include wounds that never fully heal, trauma, disabling
beliefs, low self-esteem, ego expectations and fear. The emotions
associated with these experiences and mindsets remain imprisoned
in mind/body energy. These embedded emotions can be healed by
tiger medicine, which is simply a term to express the holistic healing
the tiger spirit animal symbolizes.

The Ten of Scrolls is prescriptive. The tiger invites you to reclaim the
power that defines her role as a spirit guide. Tiger medicine applies
awe-inspiring power and healing balm to the pain and fear affecting
your energy signature.

As Holly noted, intention is everything. You can improve your
energy signature by making changes in your environment such as
people, activities, habits or boundaries, or by creating a permanent
disconnect with the negative energy that confines you. Both means
are effective. Intention and desire are then brought into balance with
your energy signature and you can break the cycle.

THE THEORY OF THE TROUPE

No one saves us but ourselves. No one can and no one may.
We ourselves must walk the path. ~ The Buddha

The Troupe makes sure that you never walk the path alone. These sixteen players, who are also archetypes, are Chrysalis' replacements for tarot's traditional Court Cards. There are eight male characters and eight female characters divvied up into four roles: Mentors, Muses, Mystics and Messengers. When you encounter Troupe members in real life, they may be represented by either sex.

Collectively, the Troupe are a band of medieval troubadours that travel the countryside bringing news and gossip from afar along with pithy wisdom and amusing entertainment. The members of the Troupe can be interpreted in a variety of ways in readings. They might represent real people—friends, family or complete strangers that you encounter on your path—or they can represent personality traits that nuance less obvious aspects of a reading.

Among the sixteen cards, you should choose at least one Troupe member to represent you. This card symbolizes the way you see yourself. There's also at least one card that represents your guardian spirit or angel. You may have more than one.

Troupe players are cunning folk gifted in the practice of magic. All Troupe members have animal familiars that also nuance readings with shamanic healing properties. For example, the Companion's familiar is the kookaburra bird native to Australia. Kookaburras chirp in an amusing birdsong that sounds like laughter. In readings, this suggests the Companion may think you're being too serious. In the Troupe card descriptions to follow, we mention the *spirit animal* attributes of all sixteen Troupe familiars.

The Troupe was designed to increase appreciation of the fact that the Otherworld sends important messages to us through other people.

The word *angel* actually means messenger. When you meet a member of the Troupe on your journey, you very well could be meeting an angel in disguise.

The Troupe's brand of magic is synchronicity. There is a truism about the Hero's Journey: whatever your needs, they will be given to you by someone at the appropriate time. You never have to ask. This might be a book, a talisman, a spiritual object, sage advice or any number of things that add meaning and purpose to your quest.

As you get to know the Troupe players, and as they get to know you, we think you'll find them gentle, helpful and wise. Remember, we don't decode Chrysalis spreads by rote, we engage in conversations with the Otherworld. At first, this approach may seem as daunting as a foreign language. But have no fear; intuition and imagination are humanity's common tongue. We have just forgotten how to speak it.

As the Mime frequently puts it, "A tarot spread is the telephone, not the conversation."

The three most important things you need to learn about each Troupe member are:

- Personality traits
- Role (Mentor, Muse, Mystic or Messenger)
- Animal familiar

THE MINSTREL
Mentor of Stones

The Minstrel was the first character of our wandering Troupe that I painted. After finding a decorative arch to serve as a repetitive motif for all Troupe cards, I began the process that paired each of our characters with an animal guide. I immediately envisioned a faithful canine companion at the heels of our singing Minstrel. It just so happened that Toney's best pal is a handsome Australian Shepherd named Ozzie. He fit the bill perfectly! With his one black eye and obvious charm, he is a favorite of Chrysalis fans everywhere.

The Minstrel's dog familiar is a humble, at times even shy fellow. And like the unassuming Minstrel, he relishes making new friends and spending time with them.

All four Chrysalis mentors are unassuming. They wouldn't be very helpful if they were overbearing or offputting. The Minstrel calls attention to worldly matters such as finance and mind and body issues that have a bearing on your physical well-being. The Minstrel is a gentle soul whose relaxing music provides a healing touch.

His dog symbolizes harmonious living with the material and spiritual worlds, the two worlds we inhabit. For us, this is not an easy task. The Minstrel's familiar goes on the road with the Troupe, but as a working dog he, too, requires help in finding meaning and purpose. Otherwise he feels misplaced. In readings, the Minstrel helps you discover spiritual meaning and purpose in a world that undervalues it.

THE ARTISTE
Muse of Stones

Needless to say, the Artiste is dear to my heart! My inspiration for her was Jacques-Louis David's portrait of Charlotte Dogne, a very atmospheric painting of a young girl in a beautifully sunlit room. The butterfly seemed the perfect companion for our artiste. Chrysalis by its very definition indicates a preparatory or transitional state. Here we are presented with a magical trio of transitions: the artiste painting, the birth of the butterfly, and the personal growth one experiences with Chrysalis Tarot.

It's only fitting that the Muse of Stones is an artist. As a group, *artiste*s include singers, dancers and even writers. In fact, all nine Greek muses would be called *artistes* in the Chrysalis vernacular. An artiste creates beauty for beauty's sake. A muse generates creative energy that inspires that beauty.

The Artiste may symbolize a real person or she may represent a spiritual force in your life that compels you to create for your own enjoyment and for others as well. Artistes are natural healers. Their beautiful creations, unique knowledge, or adept skill in the performing arts, focus the mind's eye on the present moment. Beauty steals attention from the ruminating efforts to fix past problems, which is wasted energy.

As spirit guide and familiar to the Artiste, the butterfly symbolizes an ability to appreciate beauty from many perspectives. Butterfly eyes cast a thousand lenses of joy on readings to help you appreciate the beauty that surrounds the present moment.

THE ILLUSIONIST
Mystic of Stones

Finding an inspiration figure for the Illusionist took quite some time. I was hoping to find a pose that put people in mind of a Renaissance magician with the elegance of a more modern day version of the same. It was inevitable that the dove should serve as his animal attendant. All this research triggered a long buried memory. Years ago I had a friend who reminded me of the Illusionist. He reveled in magic tricks and practiced them on his friends. Oftentimes I was the guinea pig!

An illusionist likely reminds us of a rabbit pulled out of a hat at a magic show or of someone sawed in half. The mind certainly needs such entertainment and requires occasional distractions from reality. In fact, the mind craves distraction so much that it becomes quite adept at forging illusions. Illusion is the ego's trick to prevent you from becoming a seeker of truth.

The dove, a symbol of spiritual truth, asks you to still your mind and overcome the ego's self-serving clatter and clamor meant to divert your attention from higher matters. Ego-self is the supreme master of the material realm; Higher Self is the lowly servant of the spiritual realm.

As a mystic, the Illusionist diverts the mind's attention from illusion to spiritual truth, a catastrophe for some. Virginia Wolfe wrote, "Why, if it was an illusion, not praise the catastrophe, whatever it was, that destroyed illusion and put truth in its place?"

THE ACROBAT
Messenger of Stones

*M*y inspiration for the Acrobat's animal companion was born *many years ago in the Central Park Zoo, when I used to visit the Primate House with my father. I remember wiling away the hours watching the monkey's shenanigans! How I wished I could fly from branch to branch like those free spirited souls. What better companion for our acrobat than a dexterous monkey? One mimics the other and through mobility of thought and deed a new sense of perspective emerges.*

The Acrobat's personality is genuine and engaging. She has an effervescent approach to life that's neither serious nor flip. As one of the Troupe's messengers, when you meet up with her in your journey, as you most assuredly will, be sure to consider her perspective and inspired take on things. The Troupe's messengers in real life are often angels in disguise.

The Acrobat's monkey familiar has a trait we all would do well to take to heart. She always is keenly aware of her surroundings; she reads her environment the way we read a book. She misses nothing and therefore makes a powerful ally in solving problems using active imagination and a clear perspective.

The Acrobat and her monkey familiar bring fresh eyes to whatever dilemmas you may face. Try to identify the acrobats and angelic messengers in your life. As Proust wrote, *"The real voyage of discovery consists not in seeking new landscapes but in having new eyes."*

THE SOJOURNER
Mentor of Mirrors

Wise, insightful, well read and intuitive, my father was the inspiration for the Sojourner painting. In essence, throughout my life, he was my mentor. In my youth, we spent much of our time together visiting the Metropolitan Museum of Art. We shared a fondness for the Met's splendid collections of art and history. Perhaps my father's greatest gift was his sense of compassion. Given his love of animals, it only follows that the Sojourner's companion should be a noble steed!

A sojourner is a supremely spiritual person who gathers no moss. He's infrequently found in the same place for very long, preferring instead to roam around and spend quality time with his thoughts and inspirations. The Sojourner's motto is, "Live life one day at a time." He could be called an empath and spiritual mendicant. His familiar, the Sojourner's noble steed, helps keep him from feeling constricted or tied down.

When the Troupe makes camp, the Sojourner usually leaves for a short while to visit nearby farmhouses. If he's warmly welcomed—and he usually is—he prays peace upon the household and breaks bread with them. They share information with him about places the Troupe should go and people they should meet.

The Troupe takes this same approach in Chrysalis readings. When the Sojourner appears, he's already read your heart and understands you. So sit with him for awhile. Empaths are mentors and problem solvers. He may recommend you set aside some "me time" to roam nature with your own thoughts and inspirations.

THE WATCHER
Mystic of Mirrors

*T*he crone is perhaps the most powerful of the three faces of the goddess. An ancient wise woman, she serves as healer, shaman, wisdom-keeper and watcher. I am fascinated by this phase in a woman's life, one that honors experience and knowledge. A friend who's a local artist, writer and master craftswoman in Vermont was my inspiration for this piece. She's a remarkable soul who remains active in her 'dotage.' An owl seemed the perfect companion for such an extraordinary woman.

Among their many psychic gifts, watchers can interpret the signs and symbols found in nature. They are consummate clairvoyants with ears to hear and eyes to see what others may be unable to even imagine. The Watcher character was inspired by Marie Laveau, the Voodoo Queen of New Orleans and another extraordinary crone.

As a mystic and archetype, the Watcher and her owl encourage you to improve your *night vision* by nurturing your intuitive abilities. Like Marie Laveau, the Watcher's reputation was enhanced as much by her generous mercy and compassion for the less fortunate as by the strength of her mystical power.

The Crone archetype does have a shadow-side. Should the Watcher appear frequently in readings, she probably reminds you to keep an open mind and not allow your beliefs to become rigid and staid. It's healthy to bid farewell to those areas in life that no longer serve their original purpose. The winds of change produce enlightenment.

THE DREAMER
Messenger of Mirrors

O ne of my very favorite books is "The Rubaiyat of Omar Khayyam" with illustrations by the unparalleled Edmund Dulac. My inspiration for the Dreamer came from the book's cover illustration. Two lovers meet beneath a tree in the moonlight and revel in each other's company. I used the man's pose, and as a finale I felt a leaping tiger would make a glamorous and striking companion for such an exotic dreamer. A dream personified!

Tarot and dreaming connect the personal unconscious mind with the Collective Unconscious, whose language is symbolism. Jung taught that symbols have many connotations that imply something vague and hidden from us. The interpretation of a dream or tarot spread as influenced by the Collective Unconscious seeks to clarify what was vague and uncover what was hidden.

The Dreamer is a thoughtful, reflective and mindful interpreter of symbols. His specialty is lucid dreaming, the dream state at the threshold that separates sleep from consciousness. Lucid dreams allow the dreamer to know he is dreaming yet to influence his dreams. In readings, the Dreamer asks you to be mindful of your dreams and use tarot to help you interpret them.

The tiger familiar and full moon are symbols of the power and resonance we share with the Otherworld through dreams, tarot and active imagination. This card also has ancestral symbolism. The leaping tiger is guardian and protector of the ancestors.

THE HEALER
Muse of Mirrors

This is one of my very favorite cards. I chose honeybees for our Healer's animal companions. Honey has amazing medicinal properties and I am a great lover of bees and old-fashioned straw skeps. As for the Healer herself, there is a marvelous Medicine Woman in the enchanted Gila Canyon wilderness of New Mexico who was the inspiration for this card. She and her family practically live off the land and offer spiritual retreats in their stunningly beautiful sanctuary. Gila Canyon is truly an ancient place of healing and power.

Our Chrysalis healer is known as a "Bee Maiden," a practitioner of the ancient and sacred art of bee shamanism. Her distant ancestors in India were known as the Mountain Pramnae—wandering healers who practiced medicine using roots, herbs and magical incantations. Their secrets have been passed down from grandmother to granddaughter for generations.

To the herbal remedy practices taught by her ancestors, the Healer adds the medicinal secrets of the hive—pollen, propolis, wax, and of course honey. Bee shamans can expertly position the bee's sting on the body's energy meridians as a type of acupuncture. In fact, the art of bee shamanism is the forerunner of acupuncture.

The Healer frequently quotes from a poem by Antonio Machado: *I dreamt—marvelous error!—that I had a beehive here inside my heart. And the golden bees were making white combs and sweet honey from my old failures.*

THE COMPANION
Mentor of Spirals

For The Companion I sought a friendly sort of individual as my model. I hadn't anything in particular in mind, save the atmosphere I wanted to convey. During my quest, I happened upon a wonderful Renaissance storyteller illustration in an old fairy tale book. He seemed to impart all that I intended. In addition I added a kookaburra bird. Laughing kookaburras, known as Australia's inspirational 'Merry King of the Bush' are native to the woodlands and seemed the perfect, accessible, sidekick for the Companion.

The Companion is the Troupe's version of Merlin and the Wise Old Man archetype. The other members of the Troupe rely on the Companion as they would on a professor, grandfather or priest. His advice is always shrewd and astute, especially when it involves spiritual matters. He's always ready to lend counsel.

The Wise Old Man—an archetype represented in Chrysalis by the Companion, Merlin and Papa Legba—is the masculine equivalent of the Divine Feminine archetype. Their guru-style counsel is imparted through dreams and active imagination. The Companion is a good inspirational card to place by your bedpost overnight or under your pillow.

The kookaburra helps the Companion refrain from being too serious or impatient. Kookaburra's energy is the energy of the divine. Omens, synchronicity and inspiration walk by his side, so stay alert. The Companion and his kookaburra bird make quite an entertaining pair. Their healing energy is humor and laughter.

THE MUSE
Muse of Spirals

I thought the Muse a very lovely addition to our Troupe. She reminded me very much of my daughter Esme who has often been likened to a fawn, given her large eyes and coloring. For the Muse herself, I explored various Renaissance painters and ended up settling for the Venus figure in Botticelli's "Primavera." Like Esme, the fawn and Venus figure reminded me of the fleeting, innocent and gentle beauty that is often attributed to the ancient muses. Chrysalis has these same qualities. A single card can ignite a fire that brings about meaningful change.

It's easy to resonate with the Muse archetype because she is so unassuming and approachable. She's the one who wakes you up at odd hours with creative inspirations. Her consort, the Companion, is the Troupe's Wise Old Man. She is the Troupe's Peaceful Dove, a soft and loving reflection of the Divine Feminine.

The Muse is the mistress of our passion, although we may not have discovered what our passion is yet. If that's true, this may be because of feelings of powerless, low self-esteem or a chronic pessimistic attitude. In readings, the Muse emphasizes the need to re-create yourself by addressing any such feelings of inadequacy that bog you down.

The Muse's fawn symbolizes gentleness and innocence. It reinforces her message that you not be too hard on yourself. Nurturing child-like innocence and presenting a pleasing demeanor releases blocked second chakra energy, the seat of your passion.

THE CORSAIR
Mystic of Spirals

I *have a dear friend whose personality resembles that of the Cor-*
sair. He is humorous, bold, brazen and generous of spirit. He
looks nothing like our jaunty pirate, nor does he own a parrot, but
at the time I was painting this card he definably came to mind.
My memory of the Disney World attraction, 'The Pirates of the
Caribbean' was quite inspiring as well. Who can forget the doggie
that holds the jail cell keys in his mouth but won't relinquish them
to the desperate pirates?

Normally we don't think of pirates as mystics, but mystics are among the freest souls you'll meet, and so are pirates. They march to different drums, intuit their own guiding light and author their own principles. All great sages in history had valuable pirate-like qualities.

The Corsair hails from the Golden Age of Piracy, as does pop culture's distilled image of pirates as rum-soaked buccaneers. But the Corsair symbolizes a longing for adventure and escape we all share. He champions free souls who refuse to be bound to convention. Always keeping a good lookout, the Corsair foresees sudden and dramatic change.

The Corsair's parrot familiar keeps him alert at all times. In readings they remind you also to keep a good lookout for signs and omens. The Corsair's self-confidence may make him seem obnoxious at times, but the Troupe ignores it and depends upon him a great deal. He easily interprets subtleties others fail to grasp.

THE MIME
Messenger of Spirals

My daughter Gabrielle is the Mime in our family. Since earliest youth she has been the social butterfly, encouraging the rest of us to playact, dress up and explore the unfamiliar. Her confidence, like the ram's, allows her to 'push through' where others dare not tread and she never fails to surprise when it comes to entertaining! I thought immediately of Gabi and her love of costumes and the lime-light when I drew sketches for the Mime.

W henever the Troupe performs, those in the audience experience healing via a tangled web of emotional response. The Companion makes people laugh and forget their troubles, the Minstrel makes the eyes misty with his romantic ballads, and the Corsair captivates with tales of exotic adventures in strange lands. Whenever the Mime takes the stage, you can hear a pin drop. The Mime tells stories that heal without words.

Silence is the art of the soul. The famous mime, Marcel Marceau, said his goal was always to *"reveal the inside of the Self and the depth of our feelings."* In readings, the Mime sheds "gleams of light on the shadow of man startled by his anguish." The Mime expresses the healing balm of an archangel that touches everyone.

The bighorn sheep's spiral horns symbolize creative energy, endurance and a little stubbornness. The Mime's sheep familiar reminds you not to become a "battering ram" by clinging to a point. Great power and wisdom are communicated with silence. Marcel Marceau offered this sage advice, *"Sometimes it's good to shut up."*

THE POET
Mentor of Scrolls

The gentleman who inspired my painting of the Poet lives in Ireland. Astute and erudite, almost every tidbit he's written me has enriched my being. He is one of those rare folk whose 'turn of phrase' is indisputably divine. I was so enthralled by his faculty that I began to write poetry too! I gave our Chrysalis Poet a rabbit because they are delightful companion animals. I myself had a black bunny ages ago named Paloma. The soft and gentle Paloma used to keep me company late into evenings while I painted.

Most all categories of creative writing produce healing; this is one reason Chrysalis recommends that you journal your readings. The Poet's gift of words assists you in developing metaphorical thinking. He encourages you to interrupt your routine and create time to be alone with yourself and nature.

Sweet is the lore which Nature brings;
Our meddling intellect
Mis-shapes the beauteous forms of things:—
We murder to dissect.

Enough of Science and of Art;
Close up those barren leaves;
Come forth, and bring with you a heart
That watches and receives.

—From *The Tables Turned,* by William Wordsworth, 1798

Spending time with nature is healing, as is poetry. They increase self-esteem, self-awareness and help you value contemplation. The Poet is a strong advocate of the interior life. His rabbit familiar always stays alert and aware of his surroundings. Both remind you that thoughts, emotions and intentions compose the poetry of your reality.

THE WEAVER
Muse of Scrolls

I identify with the Weaver. She works by candlelight; the scent of wildflowers and a lovely melody fill the air. Atmosphere is important to her. The Weaver is quiet and reflective in her approach, paying attention to detail and employing a methodical approach to creation. In fact I have often thought of my paintings as tapestries of design, color, detail and light. And down through the years there has always been a kitty cat by my side.

Weaving is an attribute of all Mother Goddesses that symbolizes the sutras woven into creative tapestries of energy, ideas and wisdom. *Sutra* is Sanskrit for the thread that connects all things. In Chrysalis Tarot, sutras connect you to your destiny, your family and your ancestors.

The Chrysalis Weaver is named Clotho after one of the three Greek Fates. Like all Troupe members, she may represent an important person in your life, an ancestor, a particular aspect of your personality that's blossoming, or trying to blossom, or she may inspire a fresh new perspective. Weavers have a knack for noticing small, obscure details and understanding how they seamlessly mesh with the larger reality.

Clotho's cat teaches sutras of mystery and magic that regard worldly attachments as obstacles to spiritual growth and the quality of your consciousness. It's understood that a cat's field of energy rotates opposite to that of humans and therefore cats produce a calming effect on us that neutralizes negative energy and restores balance.

THE VISIONARY
Mystic of Scrolls

The movie "Eat, Pray, Love" inspired Toney and me to create our Visionary along similar guidelines as the wonderful spiritual healer from Bali in the film. My own personal feeling is Toney is quite a Visionary himself given his achievement with Chrysalis. Memories of my marvelous trip to Bali some years ago danced through my mind as I painted this piece. Especially notable were the many colorful birds and flowers I encountered there.

The Balinese healer Ketut probably made an impression on anyone who read the book or saw the film. Should synchronicity introduce a Ketut-style visionary into your circle of friends, his message will address the need to rise above limitations of ego's rationalized theories and seek truth and harmony. A Balian is a traditional healer who regards disease as the result of disharmony.

The cosmology of the Balians is similar to Chrysalis' cosmology. Harmony needs to reign supreme on three levels: thoughts and emotions (Self), the environment (Gaia) and the Otherworld (Spirit) or illness might ensue. The Visionary's vocation is to divine sources of disharmony and restore wellness by restoring harmony to all three levels.

In readings, the Visionary's intelligent, adaptable and chatty myna bird advises to be open and honest with like-minded friends and freely discuss any disharmony present in your life. Like the Balians, non-judgmental friends and family can be of great assistance in helping overcome disease causing disharmony.

THE PILGRIM
Messenger of Scrolls

*I*nterestingly the final member of the Troupe is the Pilgrim, leading me to believe that Chrysalis has come full circle. The Pilgrim
reminds me that the journey of discovery and rebirth can always
begin anew. I chose the llama as her totem animal as it's exotic
and slightly unfamiliar. All changes in our lives feel unfamiliar
until we grow into them and Chrysalis is all about growth and
positive change!

One of the most exciting ways to experience spiritual growth is with pilgrim spirituality. It involves hardships, self-doubts, a restless unknowing, an honest self-reckoning and a substantial degree of trust in your intuition and instincts. It's not easy to leave home with little other than a fixed itinerary and a romantic ideal and allow intuition to be your guide. In fact, it's impractical for most people.

But pilgrim spirituality is also experienced by the psyche when you're in a meditative state of consciousness. Indeed, meditative consciousness is our natural state of being until it is overtaken by anxiety, fear, ego expectation and the noise made by the structured ordeals of everyday life.

The Pilgrim's llama symbolizes inner peace and steady progress on your journey. This card reminds you if you become uneasy and realize that something in your life needs to change, it's a sign that should be welcomed. It indicates that an opportunity for growth is at hand and time to let go so you can embark on an interior pilgrimage into meditative consciousness.

THE CHRYSALIS
FAIRY RING SPREAD

Faeries are spirit beings called *devas*, a Sanskrit word that refers to nonhuman beings that exist outside what we call physical reality. In addition to fairies, other types of deva include archetypes, angels, nature spirits and elementals. In the Chrysalis schema, all devas are energy beings that inhabit the Otherworld. They communicate with us via creative imagination, intuition, dreams, and synchronicity.

This does not suggest that devas are imaginary figments of the psyche. To the contrary, they are very real! The unseen realm of spirits is connected to every aspect of life in the living universe. Consciousness pervades many realms that lie beyond physical reality. Consciousness is Akashic information and a deva is conscious information with personality and a specific vocation. We designed this Fairy Ring spread to help you meet and make friends with devas who take an interest in you.

Because fairy energy, like archetypal energy, is so important when reading with Chrysalis, this spread actively invites this form of subtle energy into our lives by tuning consciousness to the fairy channel. Separating ourselves from the spirit world deprives us of the greatest gift of the living universe—a full experience of life.

THE SPREAD

First, place the Sorceress, Morgan le Fay, who is Queen of the Fairies, in what will become the center of a five-card set arrangement. Next, place Storyteller above Morgan and the Nine of Mirrors below Morgan. The Tree of Life pictured on the Nine of Mirrors grounds this spread. Storyteller becomes an antenna for the Fairy Channel and Morgan as its significator tunes the spread to fairy energy.

On either side of Morgan place one of the Chrysalis fairy-energy cards. (These cards are listed below.) Select the two that most appeal to you, or best represent issues you want the reading to address. You should now have a five-card layout in the shape of a cross to begin communication with the Fairy Realm. Next, you draw up to four cards to represent the Fairy Realm's response to your query.

CHRYSALIS FAIRY ENERGY CARDS

Elpi	Five of Stones	Ten of Stones
Six of Mirrors	Four of Spirals	Four of Scrolls
Six of Scrolls	Nine of Scrolls	

ACKNOWLEDGMENTS

This book is the product of personal experiences during more than thirty years of studying spirituality and consciousness. During those years, I received invaluable encouragement and support from many. It is often said that on a spiritual journey one always runs across those people who make certain your journey stays on course and that you discover old maps that lead to new, undiscovered treasures.

Truth, perhaps, is the greatest treasure of all. I discovered, however, that truth was not as cut-and-dry or as objective as I foolishly believed in the salad days of my first 50 years. Indeed, truth has revealed itself to be a moving target, or as Hemingway wrote "a movable feast," wrapped in mystery and magic, toil and trouble.

Holly Sierra and I designed Chrysalis Tarot to be an old map that would help our readers discover one of truth's rabbit trails; to think more critically, and to remain more open to new perspectives and possibilities. This can be difficult in cultures browbeaten with irrational and contradictory doctrines and dogmas both scientific and religious. We hope Chrysalis Tarot eases that burden and helps you experience a rational spirituality. The unseen world is an exciting place that should be experienced rather than taught.

One such rabbit trail is known as New Science. Greater understanding of quantum physics, Theory of Mind and even of consciousness itself is boldly leading civilization into a new world that is very unlike the world we grew up in. It was in that old, mechanical, material, reductionist world, that we were taught what have become outmoded worldviews. We all hate change, but we all should adapt to new truths.

We would like to acknowledge some cutting-edge scientists and critical thinkers who have contributed greatly to the fledgling theory of a connected universe, as well as to the spiritual foundations of Chrysalis Tarot. Among them are Nassim Haramein, Rupert Sheldrake, Graham Hancock, James Lovelock, Bruce Lipton, Michael Talbot, Dean Radin, Ervin Laszlo, Marc Seifer, Stanislav Grof, Russell Targ, Charles Tart, and, of course, C.G. Jung and Joseph Campbell. We commend their voluminous writings to your own musings and wanderings through the still mostly unmapped frontiers of New Science.

Holly and I would personally like to thank our editor, Lynn Araujo, and the professional staff at U.S. Games Systems who strive to make writing and painting, sometimes referred to as "getting naked in public," so enjoyable and emotionally rewarding.

I am honored to dedicate this book to my mother, Mary London, who nurtured my creative imagination. When I was five we would nuzzle up in lazy Florida sunshine and study the shapes of clouds. She would point out the puffy white elephants, beautiful castles and assorted airborne beasts as they slowly wafted by. I soon learnt to see these marvels clearly for myself.

Speaking of elephants—and because Chrysalis Tarot is such an Earth-centered, environmentally conscious deck—Holly and I would especially like to salute the extraordinary efforts of Lek Chailert and her saintly team at Thailand's Elephant Nature Park and the Save Elephant Foundation. They help make our planet a better, more compassionate place—www.saveelephant.org. Please consider a donation to this most wonderful and worthy cause.

Namaste.

Toney Brooks

I would like to acknowledge all the wonderful people that I've met on my journey as Chrysalis' artist. I must admit I had no idea how far-reaching or magical the connections would be. I also want to acknowledge my darling daughters Gabrielle Victoria and Esme Linda and my parents James and Linda Murphy. Thanks to everyone who has embraced Chrysalis and especially the wonderful folks at U.S. Games and my author Toney Brooks! Blessings!

Holly Sierra

ABOUT THE AUTHORS

TONEY BROOKS

Metaphysician and former broadcast executive Toney Brooks was born and raised in Alabama and currently resides in the U.S. Heartland. He has also lived in Italy and the former Yugoslavia, as well as Cornwall, UK, where he published a West Country tourism book about King Arthur. He studied, both formally and informally, a number of metaphysical subjects including comparative mythology, philosophy of history, and an obscure area of theology known as Mariology. He holds a PhD in Metaphysics and a certification in Spiritual Counseling.

HOLLY SIERRA

Holly Sierra has been drawn to all things mystical and magical since her childhood. Her vibrant paintings allow us a glimpse into an enchanted world filled with goddesses and mythological creatures. Holly's infatuation with Tarot began when she was a teen and discovered an antique deck amongst her parents' possessions. The Chrysalis Tarot deck is dedicated to both her beloved parents. After pursuing a fine arts education, Holly lived and traveled extensively in Asia. Multicultural themes influence her artwork, which has appeared in children's books, magazines and greeting cards. Holly makes her home in Sedona, Arizona. Her website is www.hollysierra.com.